THE SOLAR SYSTEM

OUT OF THIS WORLD WITH SCIENCE ACTIVITIES FOR KIDS

DELANO LOPEZ

ILLUSTRATED BY JASON SLATER

Other space science titles from Nomad Press

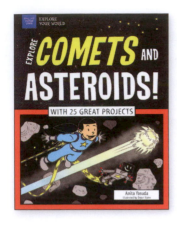

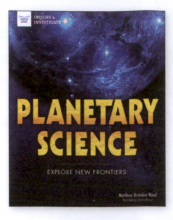

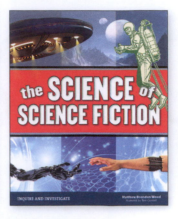

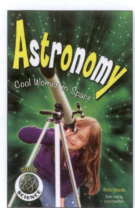

Check out more titles at www.nomadpress.net

Nomad Press
A division of Nomad Communications
10 9 8 7 6 5 4 3 2 1

This book was manufactured by CGB Printers,
North Mankato, Minnesota, United States
June 2019, Job #268930

ISBN Softcover: 978-1-61930-797-1
ISBN Hardcover: 978-1-61930-794-0

Educational Consultant, Marla Conn

Questions regarding the ordering of this book should be addressed to
Nomad Press
2456 Christian St.
White River Junction, VT 05001
www.nomadpress.net

Contents

Interested in Primary Sources?

Look for this icon. Use a smartphone or tablet app to scan the QR code and explore more! Photos are also primary sources because a photograph takes a picture at the moment something happens.

You can find a list of URLs on the Resources page. If the QR code doesn't work, try searching the internet with the Keyword Prompts to find other helpful sources.

🔎 solar system

VENUS

Discovery Date: Unknown

Discovered by: Ancient Peoples

Distance from Sun: 0.723 AU

Length of Year: 243 Earth Days

Length of Day: 224.7 Earth Days

Mass: 0.815 Earths

Diameter: 7,521 Miles
(12,104 Kilometers)

Gravity: 0.907 times Earth Gravity

Atmosphere: Carbon Dioxide

Moons: None

MARS

Discovery Date: Unknown

Discovered by: Ancient Peoples

Distance from Sun: 1.52 AU

Length of Year: 687 Earth Days

Length of Day: 24.7 Hours

Mass: 0.107 Earths

Diameter: 4,220 Miles
(6,792 Kilometers)

Gravity: 0.377 times Earth Gravity

Atmosphere: Carbon Dioxide

Moons: 2

JUPITER

Discovery Date: Unknown

Discovered by: Ancient Peoples

Distance from Sun: 5.2 AU

Length of Year: 11.9 Earth Years

Length of Day: 9.9 Hours

Mass: 317.8 Earths

Diameter: 88,846 Miles
(142,984 Kilometers)

Gravity: 2.36 times Earth Gravity

Atmosphere: Hydrogen, Helium

Known Moons: About 67

You are here.

MERCURY

Discovery Date: Unknown

Discovered by: Ancient Peoples

Distance from Sun: 0.387 AU

Length of Year: 88 Earth Days

Length of Day: 58.6 Earth Days

Mass: 0.050 Earths

Diameter: 3,032 Miles
(4,879 Kilometers)

Gravity: 0.378 times Earth Gravity

Atmosphere: Traces of Hydrogen,
Helium, Oxygen

Moons: None

EARTH

Discovery Date: Unknown

Discovered by: Ancient Peoples

Distance from Sun: 1 AU

Length of Year: 365 Earth Days

Length of Day: 24 Hours

Mass:
5,973,600,000,000,000,000,000,000
Kilograms

Diameter: 7,926 Miles
(12,756 Kilometers)

Gravity: 1: Earth Gravity

Atmosphere: Nitrogen, Oxygen

Moons: 1

CERES

Discovery Date: 1801

Discovered by: Giuseppe Piazzi

Distance from Sun: 30.1 AU

Length of Year: 4.6 Earth Years

Length of Day: 5.3 Hours

Mass: 0.00015 Earths

Diameter: 326 Miles
(525 Kilometers)

Gravity: 0.028 times Earth Gravity

Atmosphere: Traces of Water Vapor

Moons: None

NEPTUNE

Discovery Date: 1846

Discovered by: Le Verrier, Adams, Galle

Distance from Sun: 30.1 AU

Length of Year: 163.7 Earth Years

Length of Day: 16.1 Hours

Mass: 17.1 Earths

Diameter: 30,775 Miles
(49,528 Kilometers)

Gravity: 1.12 times Earth Gravity

Atmosphere: Hydrogen, Helium

Known Moons: About 14

KEY

1 astronomical unit (AU) = About 93 Million Miles
(149,598,000 Kilometers)

PLUTO

Discovery Date: 1930

Discovered by: Clyde Tombaugh

Distance from Sun: 29.7–49.3 AU

Length of Year: 249 Earth Years

Length of Day: 6.4 Earth Days

Mass: 0.0022 Earths

Diameter: 1,473 Miles
(2,370 Kilometers)

Gravity: 0.063 Times Earth Gravity

Atmosphere: Nitrogen

Moons: 5

SATURN

Discovery Date: Unknown

Discovered by: Ancient Peoples

Distance from Sun: 9.58 AU

Length of Year: 29.4 Earth Years

Length of Day: 10.7 Hours

Mass: 95.2 Earths

Diameter: 74,898 Miles
(120,536 Kilometers)

Gravity: 0.916 times Earth Gravity

Atmosphere: Hydrogen, Helium

Known Moons: About 62

URANUS

Discovery Date: 1781

Discovered by: William Herschel

Distance from Sun: 19.2 AU

Length of Year: 83.7 Earth Years

Length of Day: 17.2 Hours

Mass: 14.5 Earths

Diameter: 31,763 Miles
(51,118 Kilometers)

Gravity: 0.889 times Earth Gravity

Atmosphere: Hydrogen, Helium

Known Moons: About 27

NOTE: Drawings of planets in this book are not to scale.

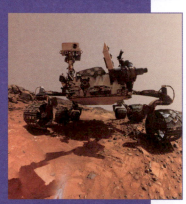

About 13.7 billion years ago. . The universe is created from the Big Bang.

About 4.6 billion years ago . . The solar system forms.

150 BCE. . . . Ptolemy writes the *Almagest*, describing the geocentric model of the solar system.

1609 CE. . . . Johannes Kepler publishes his observations in the book, *New Astronomy*, based in part on the observations of Tycho Brahe. Kepler argues that the planets travel around the sun in elliptical orbits.

1610 . . . . . . Galileo Galilei is the first to use a telescope to observe the planets. He discovers the moons of Jupiter, the rings of Saturn, and the phases of Venus.

1781 . . . . . . William Herschel discovers the planet Uranus.

1801 . . . . . . Giuseppe Piazzi discovers the first asteroid, Ceres, now considered a dwarf planet.

1846 . . . . . . The planet Neptune is discovered after both British and French teams of astronomers begin looking for a planet beyond Uranus.

1927 . . . . . . George Lemaitre develops his Big Bang theory that the universe began with an explosion at a single point.

1957 . . . . . . The Soviet Union launches *Sputnik*, the world's first artificial satellite, marking the start of the "Space Race."

1958 . . . . . . The United States launches its first satellite and forms the National Aeronautics and Space Administration (NASA).

1966 . . . . . . *Venera 3* becomes the first unmanned craft to land on another planet, Venus.

1969 . . . . . . *Apollo 11* astronauts Neil Armstrong and Buzz Aldrin land on the moon.

1971 . . . . . . The *Mars 3* lander is the first unmanned craft to land on Mars.

1977 . . . . . . The *Voyager 1* spacecraft is launched to study the outer planets, passing Jupiter in 1979 and Saturn in 1980.

1986 . . . . . . *Voyager 2*, also launched in 1977, flies close to Uranus and discovers 10 of its moons.

2006 . . . . . . Pluto is reclassified as a dwarf planet.

2008 . . . . . . The *Phoenix Mars* lander arrives safely on Mars and finds evidence of ice.

2009 . . . . . . The *Kepler* spacecraft begins its mission to search for planets outside of our solar system. As of 2017, it has discovered more than 4,000 exoplanets.

2010 . . . . . . SpaceX becomes the first private company to launch a satellite into space.

2011 . . . . . . NASA launches a car-sized robot called *Curiosity* to explore Mars. As of 2019, it is still exploring and sending images back to Earth.

2011 . . . . . . The space shuttle *Atlantis* is the last shuttle to be launched into space.

2012 . . . . . . SpaceX becomes the first private company to resupply the *International Space Station*.

2014 . . . . . . The *Rosetta* space probe becomes the first spacecraft to enter a comet's orbit, and the *Philae* lander becomes the first spacecraft to land on a comet.

2015 . . . . . . *Dawn* is the first spacecraft to enter the orbit of a dwarf planet when it orbits Ceres.

2015 . . . . . . After nine years, the *New Horizons* spacecraft arrives at Pluto.

2016 . . . . . . After a five-year journey, the *Juno* spacecraft arrives at Jupiter.

2018 . . . . . . The *OSIRIS-REx* spacecraft arrives at the asteroid Bennu and is expected to bring a sample back to Earth in 2023.

OUR
SOLAR SYSTEM

Have you ever stared up at the night sky? You likely saw a fantastic light show with stars twinkling above and the moon shining like a spotlight. Maybe you wished that you could stand on the moon. Or perhaps you thought how amazing it would be to visit another planet.

Our **solar system** is made up of planets, moons, and many other types of space objects. If they're so far away, how do we learn about them? In ancient times, people made up stories to explain how the stars, moon, and sun moved in the sky. The ancient Egyptians told myths about Re, the sun god. He sailed across the sky each morning bringing light to the world. The Japanese saw the sun as the goddess Amaterasu Omikami. The Norse believed that the sun and moon rode in chariots through the sky.

ESSENTIAL QUESTION

What is the solar system and how does it impact you?

WORDS TO KNOW

planet: a large body in space that orbits the sun and does not produce its own light. There are eight planets.

solar system: the sun, the eight planets, and their moons, together with smaller bodies. The planets orbit the sun.

civilization: a community of people that is advanced in art, science, and government.

celestial object: a star, planet, moon, or other object in space, such as an asteroid or comet.

astronomer: a person who studies the stars, planets, and other objects in space.

Anasazi: an ancient civilization of the American Southwest.

astronomical: having to do with astronomy or the study of space.

solar eclipse: when the moon passes between the sun and the earth.

astrolabe: a tool used for calculating the altitude of objects in the sky.

probe: a spaceship or other device used to explore outer space.

rover: a slow-moving vehicle used to explore planets.

universe: everything that exists, everywhere.

galaxy: a collection of star systems.

Ancient stargazers had to rely on their eyes to observe the night sky. Some **civilizations** built structures to better track **celestial objects**, including the movement of the sun. Maybe you've heard of Stonehenge or Chichen Itza.

Many ancient **astronomers** also kept records of what they saw. For example, the **Anasazi** civilization of the southwest United States observed the cycles of the sun and the moon. Their observations could have helped them mark the change of the seasons. And ancient Chinese astronomers began keeping records of **astronomical** events, such as **solar eclipses**, more than 3,000 years ago!

Much later, people used math and science to explain the stars and the planets. They also designed astronomical tools. The Greeks used **astrolabes** to figure out the position of the stars. In the 1600s, astronomers in Europe began using telescopes to see objects in the sky more clearly.

Now, teams of scientists, engineers, astronomers, and astronauts from all over the world study the solar system. They gather information about space with advanced tools and machines, including powerful telescopes, fast rockets, space vehicles, computers, **probes**, and robotic **rovers**.

DID YOU KNOW?

The word *astronomical* comes from the word *astronomy*, which is the study of the solar system and outer space. Astronomical means related to the science of astronomy, but it also means huge, vast, or inconceivably large.

An artist's rendition of a rover on Mars
credit: NASA/JPL/Cornell University, Maas Digital LLC

WHAT WE'VE LEARNED

Every person you know and every place you have ever been is located within a very small segment of the **universe** called the solar system. The solar system is massive compared to you, your backyard, or even Earth itself. But the solar system is tiny compared to the size of our **galaxy** and minuscule compared to the entire universe!

So, what is the solar system? What separates the solar system from the rest of the universe? What makes it a system of connected parts?

WORDS TO KNOW

gravity: a force that pulls all matter together, including planets, moons, and stars.

asteroid: a small rocky object orbiting the sun. Asteroids are too small to be planets.

comet: a small, icy object formed in the outer solar system that can emit tails of gas and dust if it approaches the sun.

meteor: a rock or chunk of ice that falls toward Earth from space. Small meteors burn up before they reach Earth and we see them as shooting stars.

orbit: the path an object in space takes around a star, planet, or moon.

astronomical unit (AU): a unit of measure used in space. One AU is the average distance from the earth to the sun, 93 million miles.

Most simply, the solar system is defined by the sun and its **gravity**. Everything held in place around the sun by its gravity is part of the solar system. The term *solar system* comes from the word *Sol*, the Latin name for our sun. The rest of the solar system is all the planets, **asteroids**, **comets**, and **meteors** that are held in **orbit** around the sun by its gravitational pull. It also includes the moons and rings that orbit the planets.

The sun is the reason our system works together.

Without the sun, the solar system would not exist. The sun is a star. It is only one of more than 100 billion stars in our home galaxy, the Milky Way.

The Milky Way galaxy

credit: ESO/Y. Beletsky (CC BY 3.0)

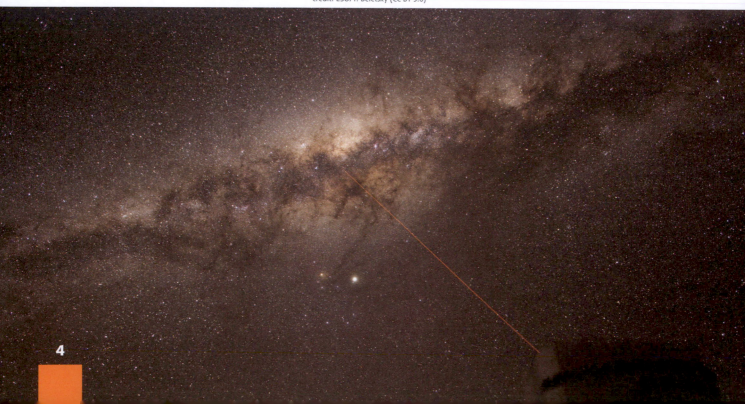

MEASURING SPACE

Space is humongous. When we measure distances on Earth, we use units of measurement such as feet and miles, or meters and kilometers. But outer space is so large that we must use larger units of measurement to easily communicate the distances between objects in space. When scientists look at objects within the solar system, they use the **astronomical unit (AU)**.

One AU is about 93 million miles. This is the average distance from the earth to the sun. The earth is one AU from the sun. Imagine driving a car to the sun 24 hours a day at 60 miles an hour. How long do you think it would take you? The answer might surprise you. It would take you more than 176 years to get there!

The distance from the sun to Jupiter is more than five times the distance from the sun to the earth, or 5 AU. You would have to travel almost the same distance again to reach Saturn, which is a little more than 9 AU from the sun. Uranus and Neptune are even farther away. Uranus is 20 AU from the sun. Neptune is another 10 times the distance from the sun to the earth past Uranus, or 30 AU.

Oort Cloud: a huge collection of comets that orbit around the outer regions of the solar system.

light-year: the distance light travels in one year, about 5.9 trillion miles.

In this book, you'll learn more about the sun that anchors our solar system in place and investigate our galaxy and objects beyond it. You will discover the history of astronomy and learn about the tools people use to study space. Plus, you'll build and test launchers, telescopes, and much more.

Let's go—the countdown clock is ticking! It's time to be launched into *The Solar System: Out of This World with Science Activities for Kids.*

Good Science Practices

Every good scientist keeps a science journal! Scientists use the scientific method to keep their experiments organized. Choose a notebook to use as your science journal. As you read through this book and do the activities, keep track of your observations and record each step in a scientific method worksheet, like the one shown here.

Question: What are we trying to find out? What problem are we trying to solve?
Research: What is already known about the problem?
Hypothesis/Prediction: What do we think the answer will be?
Equipment: What supplies are we using?
Method: What procedure are we following?
Results: What happened? Why?

Each chapter of this book begins with an essential question to help guide your exploration of the solar system. Keep the question in your mind as you read the chapter. At the end of each chapter, use your science journal to record your thoughts and answers.

ESSENTIAL QUESTION

What is the solar system and how does it impact you?

AN ASTRONOMICAL UNIT

Put on your detective hat! You will investigate how large an astronomical unit is in this activity. This activity works best outside.

❯ **First, make a model of the sun.** Find your favorite recipe for papier-mâché online. Cover your workspace with newspaper and inflate a large balloon. Mix the water and flour in a large bowl to make a papier-mâché paste. Tear some newspaper into strips and then, one by one, dip them in the paste. Lay the strips of paper on the balloon, using your fingers to smooth out the paper until the balloon is entirely covered, except for where you blew up the balloon. Tie a piece of string around the end of the balloon and let it dry out upside down. This could take several days.

❯ **Take a small ball, such as a ping-pong ball, and, using blue and green markers,** roughly draw the continents and oceans on it. Glue your Earth model to the top of a stick.

continued next page →

Where Does It End?

Just how big is the whole solar system? Many scientists agree that any object that orbits the sun is part of the solar system. The edge of the solar system would then extend to the **Oort Cloud**, which lies up to 100,000 AU from the sun. When we get outside the solar system, we must use even larger units of measurement. The main unit of measurement outside the solar system is the **light-year**. The light-year is the distance that light travels in a year, which is 186,000 miles per second. This is almost 670 million miles an hour. It takes light only about eight minutes to travel the 93 million miles (1 AU) from the sun to the earth. The nearest star, Proxima Centauri, is about 4.2 light-years away.

 It can be hard to wrap your head around the enormous size of space and the distances between things in space. **Try this video for some comparisons. Can you spot the Minecraft world?**

🔍 Scale of Universe video

Activity

❯ **Once your sun model is dry, paint it yellow like the sun.** After the paint dries, deflate the balloon at the spot you left uncovered. Attach the sun to the top of another stick.

❯ **Fill two buckets halfway with sand and go outside to a large field.** If it is a football field, place one bucket at the goal line. Push the stick with the sun model into the sand in this bucket so it stands up straight.

❯ **Take the other bucket of sand and place it halfway between the 28th and 29th yard lines, on the opposite side of the field.** Push the stick with the earth model into the sand in this bucket. The goal is to have 71.5 yards between the earth and sun models. If you don't have either a football or soccer field marked out, you can measure the distance with a measuring tape. You need a total distance of 244 feet, 6 inches between your sun and earth.

❯ **Stand next to your earth model and look at the sun model.** Now, imagine that your earth model is the size of the earth, and your sun model is the size of the sun. The distance between the models would then be 1 AU.

Think More

Turn around, away from the sun model. Now, imagine a point 40 times that distance from the sun, past the earth. That point, on the scale of your model, would be almost 2 miles away. So, when we say that Pluto is 40 AU away from the sun, that is the kind of distance we are talking about.

Try This!

Plot where the other planets in the solar system would go using everyday objects such as plastic containers. You could use a sticky note to label the planets. In your science journal, draw a picture of the field showing the distances of the planets from the sun. You can include dwarf planets, such as Pluto, if you want.

Chapter 1

THE BIG BANG AND THE
BIRTH OF STARS

Look around at your desk, chair, this book, your school, and your friends and classmates. Everything that you see is made of matter, and all matter is made of electrons, protons, and neutrons! It's pretty amazing to think that an event that happened billions of years ago formed the matter that makes up every single thing there is now.

This is what scientists think happened. There was an event that they've called the **Big Bang**. Scientists at **NASA** estimate that 13.8 billion years ago, the entire universe began as a **dense**, hot mass of energy about the size of a pebble. Suddenly, it began to expand. In the early moments of the expansion, this energy cooled and quickly formed electrons, protons, and neutrons—the basic units of matter.

ESSENTIAL QUESTION

How did stars and planets form in the solar system?

WORDS TO KNOW

matter: what an object is made of. Anything that has weight and takes up space.

electron: a small particle that makes up atoms. It has a negative charge and exists outside the nucleus.

proton: a particle that makes up atoms. It is in the nucleus and has a positive charge.

neutron: a particle that makes up atoms. It is in the nucleus and has no charge.

Big Bang: an explosion that led to the beginning of the universe.

NASA: National Aeronautics and Space Administration, the U.S. organization in charge of space exploration.

dense: when something is tightly packed in its space.

plasma: a form of matter that is similar to gas.

electromagnetic: one of the fundamental forces of the universe. It is responsible for magnetic attraction and electrical charges.

atom: the smallest particle of matter.

element: a pure substance that is made of atoms that are all the same.

hydrogen: a colorless gas that is the most abundant gas in the universe.

helium: the second most common element in the universe after hydrogen.

lithium: a metal.

nebula: a giant cloud of gas and dust among the stars. Plural is nebulae.

oxygen: a gas in the air that people and animals need to breathe to stay alive.

carbon: an element found in all living things.

At this point, all the matter in the universe was still in the form of **plasma**. A few hundred thousand years later, the universe cooled down enough so that the **electromagnetic** attraction between protons, electrons, and neutrons allowed them to join, forming **atoms**. In the early years of the universe, only the lightest and simplest **elements** were created—**hydrogen**, **helium**, and a small amount of **lithium**. What happened next was pretty amazing—stars formed!

STARS ARE BORN

A sky full of stars is one of the most beautiful sights in the world. But how did that starscape get there?

The process was all a part of the Big Bang.

Once the atoms cooled, these simple elements—hydrogen, helium, and lithium—remained scattered across the still-expanding universe. They were not spread out evenly, but were clustered into irregular clumps. The gravity between the atoms pulled these clumps toward each other. As millions of years passed, these clumps formed into large clouds of gas and dust called **nebulae**.

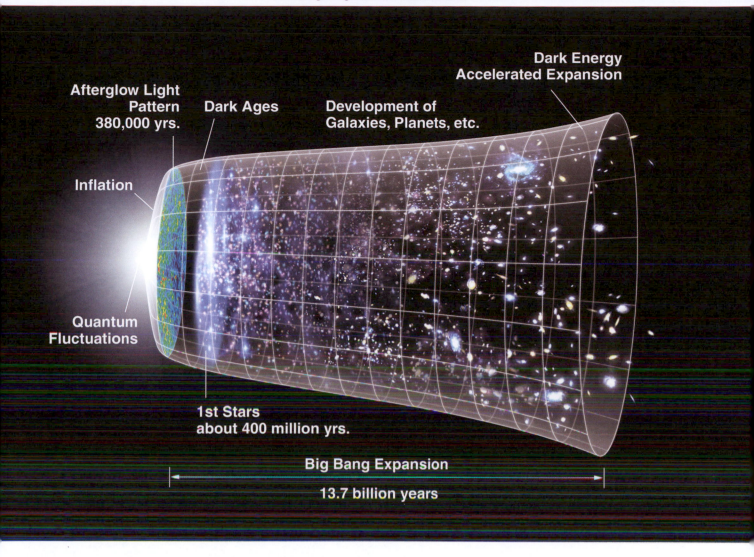

Afterglow Light Pattern 380,000 yrs.

Dark Ages

Development of Galaxies, Planets, etc.

Dark Energy Accelerated Expansion

Inflation

Quantum Fluctuations

1st Stars about 400 million yrs.

Big Bang Expansion

13.7 billion years

Scientists draw models to show what the Big Bang might have been like.
credit: NASA

A nebula can stretch for millions of miles. Most of a nebula is hydrogen, the most common element in the universe, plus some helium. A nebula also includes smaller amounts of other elements, including **oxygen** and **carbon**.

Nebulae can appear quite beautiful. The different gases in nebulae turn them different colors, and sometimes people see shapes there, just as people find shapes in the clouds over our heads. For example, two famous nebulae are called the Horsehead Nebula and the Eagle Nebula, both named after shapes people have spotted in their swirling gases.

WORDS TO KNOW

fuse: to join together under high heat.

nuclear fusion: when hydrogen fuses into helium, producing energy and light.

terrestrial planet: one of the four planets closest to the sun—Mercury, Venus, Earth, and Mars. All share characteristics with Earth.

lifespan: the average expected length of time from birth to death.

mass: the amount of matter in an object.

iron: an element that is a common metal.

silicon: a nonmetallic element found in clay and sand that is used to make computer parts.

These nebulae eventually concentrated their matter into balls of gas that were so large that the heat and pressure in the center of these balls **fused** the hydrogen atoms in their centers into helium. This **nuclear fusion** produced light and heat and created stars. These first stars, called first-generation stars, had no **terrestrial planets** around them.

Does this look like a horse's head to you?
credit: NASA

A STAR'S LIFE

Even though a star is not alive in the way that plants and animals are alive, a star has a **lifespan**. A star is born in nebulae when enough gas, mostly hydrogen, is pulled together by gravity to undergo nuclear fusion. The star can continue to fuse its hydrogen for billions of years!

But a star does not live forever. When the star stops fusing hydrogen, it dies.

Learn more about the life cycles of stars at this NASA website. What do people mean when they say we are made from the dust of stars?

🔎 NASA stars life cycle

The lifespan of a star depends upon a tug of war between two competing forces. A star's gravity works hard to collapse, or squeeze, the star into a very small and dense clump of matter. The strength of this force is proportional to the **mass** of the star. At the same time, the energetic fusion reaction of the star, which creates light and heat, pushes the star outward, fighting against gravitational collapse.

DID YOU KNOW?

For the first several million years of the universe, there were only a few elements created. There was no **iron**, **silicon**, or any of the other elements that make up the terrestrial planets. These elements would come later.

As long as the supply of hydrogen fuel for the fusion reaction lasts, the star remains stable. Once the hydrogen begins to run out, however, the star will begin to go through changes. The types of changes depend upon the size of the star.

WORDS TO KNOW

core: the center.

magnesium: an element that is abundant in nature.

supernova: the explosion of a giant star.

uranium: a naturally radioactive element.

remnant: a small, leftover piece of something.

SUPERNOVAS

Stars that are much bigger than the sun—about 10 or more times bigger—go through many changes. Once a bigger star reaches the point at which its hydrogen fusion has stopped, its gravity is so large, and creates so much pressure, that its carbon **core** fuses into other elements, such as silicon, **magnesium**, and oxygen. Eventually, some of these elements are fused into iron.

At this point, the iron gets so heavy and dense that it collapses in on itself. Then, the iron is converted into neutrons, which slam into each other so hard that they bounce back outward. This bounce slams into the last bits of hot, glowing gas that surround the star, blowing that gas outward in an explosion with amazing force. This colossal explosion is called a **supernova**. Supernovas are so bright that, to the naked eye, it might look like a new star has been created, when in fact an old star has just exploded.

DID YOU KNOW?

Nova comes from the Latin word *novus*, meaning "new."

The old star was too faint to be seen before it exploded.

The energy and heat emitted during the explosion of a supernova are so incredibly powerful that they create heavier elements than iron. Elements such as gold, silver, lead, tin, and **uranium** are formed in these explosions.

Back to the Big Bang. After a few hundred million years, some of the very largest of these first-generation stars burned up most of their hydrogen and went through the process of exploding. When these first supernovas exploded, they scattered the elements they created throughout the galaxy. The **remnants** from these supernovas flew through space and encountered remnants of other supernovas.

The Milky Way

The stars in our Milky Way galaxy look like a band of light in the night sky. Other cultures have named this bright band the Bird's Path (Finnish), the Silvery River (Chinese), the Straw Way (Turkish), and the Place Where the Dog Ran Away (Cherokee). The stars form a massive, flat disk. The disc is more than 100,000 light-years across with a bulge in the center. Spiraling out from the center are four major arms. They are called the Perseus, Sagittarius, Scutum-Centaurus, and Norma Arms. Most stars in our galaxy are born in these spiral arms.

An artist's illustration of the Milky Way
credit: NASA

Gravity eventually slowed them down and pulled them together to form new nebulae.

These new clouds of dust and gas were very similar to those out of which the first stars formed, but they had one important difference. While still mostly made of hydrogen and helium, they also had small amounts of other naturally occurring elements. It was possible for terrestrial planets made of iron, silicon, and other elements to form from these second-generation nebulae.

WORDS TO KNOW

magma: a mixture of molten, semi-molten, and solid rock beneath Earth's surface.

molten: melted into liquid by heat.

THE BIRTH OF PLANETS

Now that we've seen how stars are created, let's take a look at planets. New nebulae are pulled together by gravity until the center of the cloud gathers enough mass to become a star. At the same time, the gravitational pull causes the cloud to spin.

Imagine that you and a friend are facing each other with your arms stretched outward and your palms touching. If you were to push against each other without letting up, eventually you would fall to one side or the other.

The same thing happens with a nebula, but since the gravity keeps pulling the cloud together, it continues to spin in one direction. Spinning causes the nebula to flatten out, turning it into a mostly flat disk. This is the beginning of a solar system.

DID YOU KNOW?

In the year 1054, the SN1054 Supernova exploded. It was bright enough to be seen in daylight. Arab, Chinese, and Anasazi astronomers recorded its appearance. The cloud left over from its explosion is now known as the Crab Nebula.

The Herschel

In 2009, the European Space Agency (ESA) launched the Herschel Space Observatory. The Herschel was a telescope built to be in space. Scientists back on Earth used the Herschel to learn more about how galaxies form and change. During a four-year period, scientists used the Herschel to study hundreds of thousands of galaxies where stars form.

 PS Learn more about the Herschel and watch videos at these sites.

🔍 Herschel observatory caltech   🔍 esa activities herschel

At various points along this disk, planets began to form! About 4.5 billion years ago, in second-generation nebulae, a concentration of iron and other elements began to form about 93 million miles from the center of our solar system. This was the beginnings of the planet Earth. It was the start of the place we all call home! At other areas throughout the nebula, bits of dust and gas were pulled together, forming more planets and asteroids.

We Are All Stars

All the elements on Earth, from oxygen to iron, were produced in the core of stars. When supernovas exploded, the elements were released into space. You take in these elements when you eat, drink, and breathe—and turn them into the cells of your body. So, you and everyone you know are made from the stars that exploded billions of years ago. You are made of stardust!

Earth's creation wasn't a calm process.

Gravity pulled bits of iron and silicon dust together until they formed larger and larger concentrations of elements. They spun around the center of the cloud at high speeds.

The solar system had many spinning rocks. These rocks collided, shattered, and sometimes bounced off each other. Other times, they hit with such force that they melted and fused together, forming bigger rocks. Larger and larger rocks formed, which gave them greater concentrations of gravity, causing them to pull each other together with even more force. An ocean of **magma** probably covered the surface of the earth at this time because of the energy from all these impacts. These collisions added both mass and energy to the newly formed planet.

This period occurred approximately 4.1 to 3.8 billion years ago and was called the Late Heavy Bombardment. The earth still has a **molten** core partly because of the leftover heat and energy from that time.

THE SUN

Now, we've got stars and planets in our galaxy. And eventually, at least one of those planets will end up teeming with life—Earth! But why did life develop on Earth? We are all here because of the sun.

Just like the other stars in our solar system, the sun was made because of nuclear fusion. The sun appears brighter to us than other stars because of the distance Earth is from the sun.

The 93 million miles between this planet and that star make a world of difference when it comes to life.

DID YOU KNOW?

You don't have to worry about our sun becoming a supernova. Our sun is not big enough for that to happen. Our sun does have a lifespan and will eventually "burn out," but in a less spectacular way.

Earth enjoys a **temperate** climate, a breathable **atmosphere**, and liquid water. This is because of the distance between the earth and the sun, and all of those things mean that life can thrive here.

We've learned how stars have a lifespan. What about our sun? Stars about the size of our sun go through a period of turning hydrogen into helium until most of the hydrogen in the core is used up.

Sun Protection

Yes, we need the sun for there to be life on Earth, but we also need to protect ourselves from the sun. The sun emits **ultraviolet rays** that can damage human skin. Have you ever gotten a sunburn? That's why you should wear long sleeves or sunscreen when going outside. Ultraviolet rays can also cause skin cancer. So, cover up!

The Helix nebula, a white dwarf star, shows a fate similar to that of our sun.
credit: NASA/JPL-Caltech

Once that happens, the force of gravity will overcome the weakened outward push of fusion and the star will shrink. This will increase the pressure and heat in the center of the star, causing the helium that is created by hydrogen fusion to fuse into carbon.

During this process, the star will expand and its surface will become cooler. When this happens, our sun will become a type of star called a red giant. You still don't need to worry, because this won't happen for a few billion years! After the red giant period, the sun will run out of helium to fuse into carbon. It will then collapse into a very small, very dense, ball of carbon about the volume of the earth, but many times more massive. Its surface will be quite hot and will continue giving off light and heat as it cools down, even though it will no longer be fusing one element into another. This kind of star is called a white dwarf.

After many more millions of years, it will eventually cool down completely. The planets will continue to orbit the cold sun in darkness. By then, our descendants may have spread to other star systems circling younger stars, carrying with them the life that was created in our solar system!

Now that we've seen how the universe came to be, let's take a closer look at the planets, starting with the terrestrial planets closer to the sun.

ESSENTIAL QUESTION

How did stars and planets form in the solar system?

WORDS TO KNOW

Jovian planets: a term for Jupiter, Saturn, Uranus, Neptune.

satellite: a natural or artificial object that orbits a larger object in space.

data: information, facts, and numbers from tests and experiments.

axis: an imaginary line through a planet's poles, around which it rotates. Plural is axes.

rotation: turning around a fixed point.

But the planets all share the fact that they spin on their **axes** and they orbit the sun. The time it takes for a planet's **rotation** around its axis is the length of its day. The time it takes for a planet to orbit all the way around the sun is the length of its year.

DID YOU KNOW?

Scientists have discovered water ice on Mercury!

THE TERRESTRIAL PLANETS

Mercury is the closest planet to the sun and the smallest of the four terrestrial planets. Venus comes next, but is hotter than Mercury because its dense atmosphere traps heat. Neither Mercury nor Venus has its own moon. Next in order is Earth and its moon, and then comes Mars and its two moons, Deimos and Phobos.

Mercury

credit: NASA/Johns Hopkins University Applied Physics Laboratory/Carnegie Institution of Washington

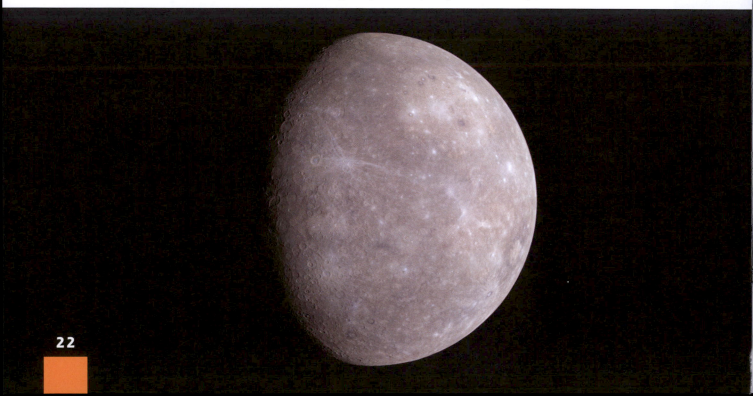

MERCURY

Mercury is the closest planet to the sun. This means it can get incredibly hot on Mercury—in the daytime, it can reach 806 degrees Fahrenheit (430 degrees Celsius)! The hottest temperature ever recorded on Earth was 134 degrees Fahrenheit in 1913 in Death Valley, California. At night, the temperature can drop to -292 degrees Fahrenheit (-180 degrees Celsius).

One reason Mercury has such extreme temperatures is because it doesn't have much of an atmosphere. The sun's heat bombards the surface of the planet during the day and then bounces back into space at night. And its days and nights are very long because Mercury spins slowly on its axis.

**One Mercury day equals 59 Earth days!
But its years are short—it takes Mercury
only 88 Earth days to orbit the sun.**

VENUS

Visit this site to learn more about living on Mercury!

PS

🔍 Space living Mercury

Venus is unusual in many ways. Every planet spins around its axis, but Venus rotates in the opposite direction of Earth and most of the other planets as it orbits the sun. Venus also rotates very slowly, even more slowly than Mercury. From sunrise to sunrise on Venus takes about 243 Earth days. Since it takes Venus about 225 Earth days to orbit the sun, a day on Venus is longer than its year!

The surface of Venus is a mystery because of the planet's thick atmosphere. But scientists know that humans could never stand on its surface. Temperatures on Venus can reach 854 degrees Fahrenheit (457 degrees Celsius), making it the hottest planet in the solar system!

WORDS TO KNOW

phenomenon: something seen or observed. Plural is phenomena.

greenhouse effect: a process through which energy from the sun is trapped by a planet's atmosphere, warming it.

evaporate: when a liquid heats up and changes into a gas.

carbon dioxide (CO_2): a gas in the air made of carbon and oxygen atoms.

crust: the outer, thin layer of the earth.

mantle: the layer of the earth between the crust and the core, the upper portion of which is partially molten.

tectonic plate: a large section of the earth's crust that moves on top of the mantle, the layer beneath the crust.

nickel: a hard, silver element.

Generally, planets in the solar system that are closer to the sun are hotter than those farther away. So, Mars is colder than Earth, and Neptune is much colder than either of them. Temperatures on Neptune can plummet to a frigid -392 degrees Fahrenheit (-236 degrees Celsius)!

Venus is one important exception to this—the surface temperature of Venus is much hotter than Mercury. How can this be when Venus is about twice as far from the sun as Mercury? Between 3 to 4 billion years ago, Venus began to absorb more energy from the sun than it could send out into space.

Venus
credit: NASA

Scientists call this **phenomenon** the runaway **greenhouse effect**. They do not yet know why Venus experienced this phenomenon. As temperatures on Venus rose, all the planet's water **evaporated** into the atmosphere. As time passed, Venus developed a thick atmosphere of greenhouse gases such as **carbon dioxide (CO_2)**. Greenhouse gases in Venus's atmosphere prevented heat from escaping into space and caused the planet to heat up.

Almost 96 percent of the atmosphere of Venus is carbon dioxide. In contrast, Mercury has very little atmosphere and it radiates energy from the sun back into space.

EARTH

Home! Most of us spend all of our time on this planet, but what's really beneath our feet? The earth is made up of three different layers—the **crust**, the **mantle**, and the core. We live on the outermost layer, the crust. On land, the crust's thickness is about 19 miles deep. Beneath the crust lies the mantle, an area 1,400 miles thick.

Scientists often compare the mantle to a chewy caramel because it's composed of molten rock.

Tectonic Plates

What we think of as solid earth is actually a thin, brittle crust floating on molten rock. This crust is further divided into moving pieces called **tectonic plates**. Tectonic plates move slowly during many millions of years. In some places on Earth, the plates run into each other, creating mountains such as the Himalayas in Asia. In others, the plates are moving apart. For example, the two plates that North America and Europe sit on are moving apart roughly 2 inches a year.

The core is about 759 miles thick and is divided into the inner and outer core. The inner core is made of solid iron and **nickel**, while the outer core is made of liquid iron and nickel.

WORDS TO KNOW

radioactive: having or producing a powerful form of energy known as radioactivity.

friction: a force that slows down objects when they rub against each other.

lava: magma that has risen to the earth's surface.

fossil: the remains or traces of ancient plants or animals left in rock.

Pangaea: a huge supercontinent that existed about 300 million years ago. It contained all the land on Earth.

volcanism: the motion of molten rock under a planet's surface, which results in volcanos.

geology: the study of the earth and its rocks. A scientist who studies geology is a geologist.

nutrients: substances in food and soil that living things need to live and grow.

climate change: a change in long-term weather patterns, which can happen through natural or man-made processes.

This outer core is molten because of the great heat within the earth. This heat comes from three sources. Some heat is left over from the time Earth formed. Other heat comes from the breakdown of **radioactive** elements such as uranium that occur naturally in the earth. The third source of heat is generated by **friction** when denser material sinks in the core.

Together, these sources of heat are hot enough to melt rock. Even though our planet appears solid, much of it is liquid. This liquid rock in the mantle is called magma. Sometimes, when the pressure and heat of the mantle gets great enough, it bursts through the crust of the planet, forming a volcano. When the hot magma reaches the surface, it is called **lava**.

Alfred Wegener

Alfred Wegener (1880–1930) was a German scientist. He wanted to know why similar plant and animal **fossils** could be found on different continents. Based on his observations, Alfred developed a theory that the continents were once joined together. He called this huge supercontinent **Pangaea**. Alfred believed that the continents drifted away from each other during a long period of time because of the way the tectonic plates move. Alfred published his ideas in 1915, but no one thought he was right. His ideas didn't gain acceptance until the 1960s, more than 30 years after his death.

Volcanism is an important factor in the **geology** of Earth. Volcanic materials provide a lot of **nutrients** to the soil. It even helps keep the atmosphere cool by releasing sulfur gas, which combines with water into droplets that prevent the atmosphere from getting too hot.

One unique thing about Earth is its atmosphere, which is a perfectly balanced mixture of oxygen, nitrogen, argon, and carbon dioxide. This mixture in the atmosphere maintains a temperature ideal for life.

The greenhouse effect is not always bad. Without the greenhouse effect, temperatures on Earth would be roughly 60 degrees Fahrenheit (16 degrees Celsius) colder. But people are adding gases to our atmosphere so fast it is causing Earth's temperature to rise. This is called **climate change**. **Watch a video by the U.S. Environmental Protection Agency about the greenhouse effect on Earth.**

PS

⌕ USEPA greenhouse video

In recent decades, this balance in atmosphere has become less and less balanced. As a result, the earth is experiencing increasingly hot temperatures. The vast majority of scientists agree that human activity, such as burning fossil fuels for energy to power our homes and cars, is to blame. All this energy production releases more and more carbon into the atmosphere, upsetting that balance. The atmosphere traps more of the sun's heat near the surface of the earth, making it hotter.

WORDS TO KNOW

water vapor: water as a gas, such as fog, steam, or mist.

science fiction: a story featuring imaginary science and technology.

MARS

The surface of Mars looks red because it has large amounts of iron. When the iron mixes with oxygen, it forms iron oxide and turns red. Mars is basically covered in rust! There are also rocks and craters. Plus, ice caps made of frozen water and frozen carbon dioxide cover both the north and south poles of this planet. Sound like a nice place to visit?

Just like Earth, Mars has volcanoes and canyons. Sometimes, planet-wide dust storms hide the surface from our eyes. Clouds can often be seen floating in the thin atmosphere of Mars.

Welcome to Mars
credit: NASA/JPL/USGS

Water Ice and Vapor

Some of the terrestrial planets and their moons have water ice and **water vapor**. In 2005, NASA launched the *Mars Reconnaissance Orbiter* (MRO). The orbiter's mission was to find evidence of water on Mars. The orbiter has found eight sites on Mars with thick ice sheets below the surface. Scientists still have many questions about these ice deposits, such as where the ice goes. Maybe you will be part of a mission that solves the mystery of ice on Mars!

A day on Mars is very similar to an Earth day in length—24 hours and 40 minutes. Its year, however, is twice as long. It takes 687 Earth days for Mars to orbit all the way around the sun. Mars has seasons that last for about five Earth months each!

People on Earth have long looked toward Mars as a place that might host life. Martians are the stuff of many **science fiction** books and movies! However, no evidence of life has yet been found on the surface of Mars, though we have found many of the elements needed for life to exist there. And researchers are still looking.

DID YOU KNOW?

The largest mountain on Mars, Olympus Mons, is an extinct volcano. Olympus Mons is more than two times as tall as the highest mountain on earth, Mount Everest.

THE JOVIAN PLANETS

Heading deeper into space away from the sun, we come to the four Jovian planets—Jupiter, Saturn, Uranus, and Neptune. These planets are very different from the terrestrial planets. For one thing, they are enormous. Jupiter and Saturn are hundreds of times the mass of Earth, while Uranus and Neptune are about 15 times Earth's mass. The Jovian planets are also called gas giants because they are mostly composed of hydrogen and helium. Let's take a look!

WORDS TO KNOW

debris: the scattered pieces of something that has been broken or destroyed.

Trojan War: a war fought between the ancient Greeks and the people of Troy around 1250 BCE.

JUPITER

Jupiter is the largest of the gas giants. It is also the second-largest object in the solar system, second only to the sun itself. In fact, the solar system has been described as the sun, Jupiter, and some **debris**, because the sun and Jupiter make up 99 percent of the total mass of the solar system! Earth and all the other planets make up only a small amount of the total mass. Jupiter has more than 300 times the mass of Earth. It is also more than three times as massive as the next largest gas giant, Saturn.

Jupiter has its own weather patterns, which are visible as colorful lines and stripes in its atmosphere. The most noticeable of these patterns is the Great Red Spot. It is a huge windstorm more than 8,500 miles across. The windstorm has circled like a hurricane in the atmosphere of Jupiter for more than 150 years. As early as the 1600s, astronomers saw a red dot with their telescopes, but modern scientists do not know if they were gazing at the same storm we can see today.

DID YOU KNOW?

The word *Jovian* comes from the word *Jove*, another name for the Roman god Jupiter.

Jupiter's Moons

Jupiter has 79 known moons, but not all of them have been named. Most of these moons are no larger than 6 miles across. And one moon, discovered in 2018, has been compared to a speck of dust—it is less than a mile across! In 1610, Italian astronomer Galileo Galilei (1564–1642) discovered four of Jupiter's moons—Io, Europa, Ganymede, and Callisto. They were the first moons discovered beyond Earth.

Watch a video taken by NASA's *Juno* spacecraft of Jupiter's four largest moons, Io, Europa, Ganymede, and Callisto.

🔎 NASA Jupiter moons

Jupiter and two of its moons
NASA/Damian Peach, Amateur Astronomer

Beneath the atmosphere of Jupiter, the gas becomes dense enough to change into a liquid. Jupiter is mostly an ocean of liquid hydrogen. It has faint rings around it, but these are not as large or as visible as the rings of Saturn.

Could you fly through a gas giant? **Find out the answer here!**

🔍 NASA Jupiter Saturn fly

Jupiter has a short day but a long year. It spins on its axis once every 9.9 hours, but takes almost 12 Earth years to orbit the sun. There are more than 10,000 days in a Jupiter year!

Jupiter shares its orbit with two large groups of asteroids known as the Trojans, named for Greek heroes in the **Trojan War**. One group of asteroids travels slightly ahead of Jupiter in its orbit around the sun. The second group of asteroids travels behind Jupiter in the same orbit.

WORDS TO KNOW

planetoid: a small celestial object resembling a planet.

SATURN

DID YOU KNOW?

All four of the Jovian planets have rings around them. Saturn's are just the biggest and most noticeable.

Saturn—famous for its large, colorful rings—is the next planet after Jupiter. Saturn's rings extend 60,000 miles from the planet. From Earth, they look like large, solid, flat disks. But Saturn's rings are not solid at all. They are made up of millions of pieces of ice and rock that clump together. Some pieces are as small as a fleck of dust, others are as large as a car. The pieces reflect light from the sun. In areas with ice, the rings appear green or blue. Areas mixed with dirt appear pink or red.

When Saturn is viewed from Earth with the naked eye, it appears to be just a bright point of light. It wasn't until people looked at Saturn through telescopes that they saw the planet's rings. But it was unclear even with these early telescopes what Saturn's rings were. They seemed to change size and shape. Sometimes, the rings appeared to be almost round. Other times, they were more stretched out. The rings even seemed to disappear at times.

Saturn's main rings are estimated to be about 30 feet thick and about 175,000 miles across. Saturn is also orbited by 62 known moons, including its largest, named Titan.

Attached Moons

In 1610, Galileo Galilei was the first person to study Saturn with a telescope. He saw Saturn's rings, but he wasn't sure what they could be. Galileo determined that they must be moons. However, when he looked at the planet a few years later, he thought maybe the moons were attached to the planet like arms.

Saturn

credit: NASA/JPL/Space Science Institute

We really got to know Saturn starting in 2004, when the *Cassini* spacecraft entered the planet's orbit and traveled close enough to take pictures and collect data on this distant planet. *Cassini* spent more than 20 years in space before its fuel ran out and the spacecraft plunged into Saturn's atmosphere, continuing to return data to scientists until it burned away.

Like Jupiter, Saturn has a short day and a long year. Because it is so far from the sun, it takes Saturn more than 29 years to complete its orbit.

Once past Saturn, the solar system seems quite empty for some distance. Between Jupiter and Neptune is a scattering of tiny **planetoids**, called Centaurs. But the planetoids are so few and small that if we were traveling between the planets, we'd be unlikely to bump into them.

What role do Saturn's moons play in the formation of the planet's rings? **Read more and see images of Saturn's rings taken** by the *Cassini* spacecraft.

PS

🔎 Cassini Saturn rings

Names of the Planets

Ancient stargazers came up with many different names for the planets. For example, the Babylonians named the five visible planets, along with the sun and the moon, after their gods.

Chinese astronomers named the five visible planets after natural elements—wood, fire, earth, metal, and water. In Mandarin, Mars is called *Huoxing*, meaning the Fire Star. Earth is called *Dìqiú*, meaning ball of earth.

The Greeks and Romans named the planets after their gods and goddesses. In English, six planet names come from the Romans and two come from the Greeks. Mercury was named for the Greek winged messenger god because Roman sky watchers observed that it moved faster than the other planets. Mercury is the fastest planet because it has the shortest orbit. Venus was named after the Roman goddess of beauty. Mars was named after the god of war because of the planet's red color. The largest planet, Jupiter, was named after the king of the Roman gods. Saturn was named for the Roman god of farming and Neptune for the god of the sea.

DID YOU KNOW?

The five visible planets are Mercury, Venus, Mars, Jupiter, and Saturn. You can see them with the naked eye if you know when and where to look.

URANUS AND NEPTUNE

Uranus and Neptune are similar in many ways. They are close in size, about 30,000 miles in diameter, though Neptune is slightly denser, and thus has a greater mass than Uranus. Both have small rings of fine particles that are easily observable from Earth. They also have many moons. Uranus has 27 and Neptune has 14.

They are called the ice giant planets, but scientists believe that Uranus and Neptune have very little solid ice. Instead, they believe that the planets have massive liquid oceans. The oceans could account for up to 85 percent of their mass.

Uranus
credit: NASA/JPL-Caltech

Astronomers have learned that the axis of Uranus is not up and down or tilted slightly, like Earth's axis. The planet is tipped on its side! Scientists think that another planet may have knocked Uranus over in the early years of the solar system. Uranus spins facing toward and away from the sun once every 17 hours. It takes the planet 84 Earth years to orbit the sun! The planet's odd rotation also affects its seasons. The north pole of Uranus has 21 years of night in the winter and 21 years of day in the summer. In the spring and fall, its north pole has 42 years of day and night.

Days on the Jovian Planets

The length of a day on each Jovian planet is different because each planet rotates at a different speed. Based on information from this site, you can compare the Jovian planets.

 You can also see pictures and watch videos to learn more about the Jovian planets.

🔎 Colorado Jovian planets

WORDS TO KNOW

indigenous: native to a place.

Indigenous peoples in North America also studied the stars and the planets. **Learn more about indigenous astronomy here.**

PS

🔍 sky stories

Unlike Uranus, Neptune is only slightly tilted on its axis. It takes Neptune 16 hours to make one rotation. Neptune's atmosphere is made up of ices and gases, including hydrogen and helium. It appears blue, with streaks of white clouds. Space probes have shown that these clouds change quickly. The *Voyager II* space probe tracked one cloud that moved around the planet every 16 hours!

Neptune also has several spinning storms that look like dark spots—similar to Jupiter's Great Red Spot. Unlike storms on Jupiter, storms on Neptune seem to form and disappear quickly, with winds reaching speeds of up to 1,300 miles per hour!

Planets are fascinating places to study, but in the next chapter we'll take a look at something a little closer to home—our moon!

ESSENTIAL QUESTION

How are the terrestrial planets and Jovian planets similar? How are they different?

Neptune

credit: NASA

TECTONIC PLATES AND VOLCANISM

Learning about the solar system can be delicious! In this activity, you will create an edible model of tectonic plates. You'll need a box of instant pudding and some brown sugar.

Caution: An adult must supervise this project.

▶ **Follow the directions on an instant pudding mix.** Place it in a heatproof dish and refrigerate the pudding for approximately 15 minutes.

▶ **Sprinkle a coating of brown sugar on top of the pudding.** Turn on the broiler to melt the sugar on top of the pudding. You want to quickly melt the sugar, and then let it cool, forming a hard crust on top of the pudding.

▶ **Gently heat the pudding on the stovetop.** The crust of sugar represents the earth's crust, while the hot pudding represents the hot mantle. What happens to the crust? The crust should break into pieces, and move about, like the tectonic plates, and bubbles of hot pudding may burst through the surface, like magma. Be careful, hot sugar or pudding can burn you! Write down your observations in your science journal. How is the sugar crust like Earth's crust? Write down ideas in your science journal.

Why are volcanoes on Mars so much larger than volcanoes on Earth?

PS **Learn more about Olympus Mons here.**

🔍 NASA Olympus Mons

Try This!

After the pudding has cooled, press down on opposite pieces of the crust while pulling them apart. Does the magma pudding flow between the pieces? Write down your observations in your science journal. What landforms do you think hot magma can form? Now, you can eat the pudding!

CREATE A GREENHOUSE

For this activity, you will grow plants to better understand how greenhouse gases temporarily trap heat in Earth's atmosphere.

❯ **Fill two small pots with potting soil.** Find some seeds that grow well in warm weather and plant them according to the directions on the packet.

❯ **Place each pot inside its own shoebox.** Label one of the boxes "Mercury" and place a thermometer inside.

❯ **Label the other box "Venus" and place another thermometer inside.** Tape four sticks in the corners of this box, sticking straight up about a foot.

❯ **To form a greenhouse around the Venus pot, stretch plastic wrap across the box and stick frame.** Secure the plastic wrap with tape or a rubber band.

❯ **Place both boxes outside in the sun.** After about 10 minutes, look at the thermometers and compare the two temperatures. Write down the results in your science journal.

Venus Express

In 2005, the European Space Agency (ESA) launched its first spacecraft—called the *Venus Express*—to study Venus. The spacecraft's mission was to study the atmosphere of Venus and measure temperatures on the planet's surface. It collected information from 2006 until 2014 with many different instruments, including one that could measure the temperature of the atmosphere. The *Venus Express* made many important discoveries, including evidence that billions of years ago, the planet had a large amount of water, just like Earth.

To learn more about the scientific instruments on the *Venus Express*, visit the ESA website.

🔍 Venus orbiter instruments

▶ **Move both plants to a location that gets some sun each day.** You will need to be able to get in and out of your "greenhouse" on Venus, so devise a system that allows you access.

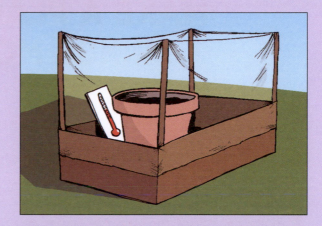

▶ **Let the seeds grow, watered and cared for as the seed packet instructs.** Make sure that whatever you do for one plant, you do for the other. Water them the same amount. And if you give one plant some plant food, give the same amount to the other.

▶ **Take measurements at least once a week.** Write down the measurements and the temperature of each box in your science journal. Make a bar graph to compare the heights and temperatures of the plants.

▶ **If you planted flowers, count the number of flowers.** Record your observations and results in your science journal.

✱ How are they different?

✱ How are they similar?

✱ How many leaves do they have?

✱ After comparing your results, what conclusions can you draw?

What's Happening?

The plastic wrap of your greenhouse keeps hot air from rising and taking away the heat. This process is called **convection**. Greenhouse gases, such as those on Venus, block the escape of heat. They allow energy in, in the form of light, but block it from leaving in the form of heat.

WORDS TO KNOW

convection: the transfer of heat from one region to another by the movement of a gas or liquid.

MAKE A PLANETARY RINGS MODEL

Ideas for supplies: clear plastic disk with a hole in the middle, glue, salt glitter in different colors, clay

Make a model of Saturn's rings to explore how the rings appear to change shape.

❯ **Place the pencil through the center of the disk so that it pokes out an inch or so on the other side.** Make sure it fits tightly while still allowing the disk to spin.

❯ **Hold the stick in one hand and gently spin the disk like a top.** While spinning, apply a small amount of glue to one point on the disk. Keep the bottle of glue still, and spin the disk, so that you make an even ring of glue.

❯ **Sprinkle your salt glitter onto the ring of glue while carefully spinning the disk.** Tap off the excess salt glitter and let the glue dry.

❯ **Repeat steps 2 and 3 as many times as you want to create many different rings.** Try using different-colored salt glitter to make different-colored rings. Shake off the excess, and let the glue dry between each repetition.

❯ **Remove the stick from the center of the disk.** Form some clay into a ball about 1½ inches in diameter. Cut the ball in half and glue one half on top of the disk in the center above the hole, and the other half to the bottom of the disk.

> **Mount your model on a stick or hang it from a string.** Turn off the lights and shine a flashlight on your model from across the room. Write down your observations in your science journal and add diagrams. Are you able to see the small particles? What happens if you look at the model directly at the edge? How could you position the model to make the rings appear larger?

DID YOU KNOW?

Most of the planets, including Earth, spin counterclockwise, from west to east. Venus and Uranus are different and spin clockwise. from east to west. In addition, Uranus is tilted so far over it spins on its side.

Try This!

The main rings around Saturn are 180,000 miles across, yet Saturn's rings are incredibly thin. The thinnest rings are only 32 feet thick. What other materials could you use to represent the thinnest of Saturn's rings? Repeat the experiment and record your observations in your science journal.

Chapter 3

EARTH'S
MOON

Sometimes, it can seem that everything in the solar system is too far away to really study it without expensive equipment. While expensive equipment does make space more accessible to scientists, there is one celestial object—the moon—that is so close, you can make observations and collect data from your own backyard!

All of the planets have moons, except for Mercury and Venus. Some planets, such as Jupiter, have lots of moons. Earth has only one moon. But it's our moon, and the only other celestial object humans have stepped foot on, which makes it pretty special.

ESSENTIAL QUESTION

How are the two types of craters made?

A CHANGING MOON

WORDS TO KNOW

wax: to get bigger.

wane: to get smaller.

What do you notice about the moon when you look at it every night at the same time for a month? Does it always look the same? Does it ever look the same?

The moon goes through phases, in which it appears to change shape. It goes through these changes during a lunar month—29.5 days. The moon does not actually change shape. Changes in the positions of the earth, moon, and sun cause the phases. As these bodies move, the moon looks different from Earth. A full moon, for example, occurs when Earth is right between the sun and the moon.

A new moon looks like a smile. It occurs when the moon is right between the earth and the sun.

When the moon appears to grow larger each night, it is called a **waxing** moon. When the moon appears to become smaller each night, it is called a **waning** moon.

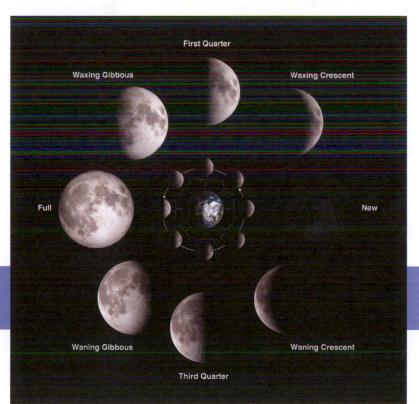

The phases of the moon
credit: NASA/Bill Dunford

CRATERS

Have you ever looked look at the moon through a telescope or even binoculars? You likely saw marks, or **craters**, on its surface. The moon's surface has millions of craters. Some of the smallest moon craters are visible only with a microscope. The largest craters are called basins. The largest moon crater is the South Pole–Aitken Basin. It is about 1,550 miles wide!

Most rocky planets, asteroids, and moons in the solar system have craters. Even the earth has lots of craters. Earth's craters are harder to see than craters on the moon because of **erosion**. Earth's surface is constantly being shaped by wind, water, and ice. The moon, however, does not have erosion. There is no wind, water, or ice to change its features.

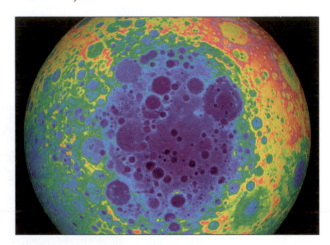

The South Pole–Aitken Basin on the moon
credit: NASA/GSFC/University of Arizona

Watch a video about mapping the surface of the moon with radar. How could these maps be used by scientists in the future?

PS

🔎 moon radar mapping

MOONS OF OTHER PLANETS

We think of our moon as pretty special—and it is—but there are more than 150 other moons out there in the solar system, orbiting other planets. We discussed some of them on our journey through the planets. Let's take a closer look at a few of the more unusual ones.

Heads Up!

There are two types of craters—impact and volcanic. An **impact crater** is formed when an object such as an asteroid slams into the surface of another object in space such as a moon, planet, or asteroid. The force of the collision leaves behind a pit or a crater. The asteroid Vesta, for example, is covered in impact craters. The largest of these craters is 325 miles wide! The largest impact crater on Earth was discovered in Australia in 2015—it's 250 miles wide! Scientists believe that the crater formed when two asteroids crashed into Earth about 300 million years ago. Volcanic explosions can create the second kind of crater. After magma bursts through the surface of a planet, the volcano collapses. The collapsed portion becomes a crater. More than 15,000 years ago, a volcano in what is now called Nevada exploded, creating a 400-acre large pit. Today, the pit is called the Lunar Crater.

Triton is Neptune's largest moon, and we've been gathering data about this natural satellite since it was discovered in 1846. Triton is the only moon that orbits in a direction that's opposite to the rotation of its planet. And this moon appears to have seasons. Another interesting fact about Triton—part of its surface appears to have been melted. Scientists believe this happened when Neptune first caught Triton in an orbit, a move that produced enough heat that the moon was liquid for a billion years.

Io, one of Jupiter's moons, would not be a good place to book a vacation. Io is one of the most volcanically active places in the solar system! This celestial object spews out more than 100 times as much lava as all of Earth's volcanoes, and Io is much, much smaller than our planet. Io has lava lakes and rivers all over it.

DID YOU KNOW? A dark area on the moon's surface is a **mare** created by asteroids. Some Western cultures see the dark areas as the face of a man. Other cultures see these spots as animals, including a rabbit and a frog.

WORDS TO KNOW

elliptical: shaped like an ellipse, or an oval.

momentum: the force that a moving object has in the direction that it is moving.

gravity well: the pull of gravity that a large object in space exerts.

DID YOU KNOW?

Neptune's moon, Neso, has the longest orbit of any moon. It takes Neso about 26 years to complete one orbit of Neptune.

One of Saturn's moons, Enceladus, is considered to be one of the most likely places to find life outside of Earth. An ocean that lies beneath the surface of Enceladus has been tested, and the chemical evidence found there suggests the existence of hot fluid vents, which are places that the planet's heat escapes through. On Earth, hot fluid vents under the sea are teeming with life. Maybe it's the same for Enceladus!

ORBITS

Planets, asteroids, and comets follow regular, **elliptical** paths called orbits around the sun. Earth orbits the sun in 365 days, or one year. Neptune, the farthest planet from the sun, takes 164 years to complete one orbit of the sun!

But moons do not orbit the sun—they orbit planets and asteroids. Why? Astronomers use Isaac Newton's (1643–1727) law of gravity to explain how planets move. An object stays in orbit because of forces working upon it. Newton's first law of motion says that an object will travel in a straight line until something acts on it.

The forces that act on planets and moons to keep them in orbit are gravity and momentum.

The gravity of two objects pulls them together, according to Isaac Newton. But, according to German scientist Albert Einstein (1879–1955), the mass of the two objects bends space and time, so a planet or star creates a **gravity well** that an orbiting planet or moon falls into.

Big Impact

Each year, thousands of rocky bits from meteors and comets enter Earth's atmosphere. Most are harmless. They burn up in the atmosphere before they ever reach the surface of our planet. However, some asteroids have made a big impact during Earth's history. One example is the Vredefort Crater in South Africa. More than 2 billion years ago, a 6-mile-wide asteroid crashed into the ground, creating a hole 10 times larger than the Grand Canyon. The Vredefort Crater is now much smaller because Earth's surface is continuously being shaped by natural processes such as erosion.

 How often do impacts occur on the moon and the earth? **Learn more about the difference between craters on the moon and the earth at this website.**

🔍 NASA moon craters

In Newton's model, gravity pulls two objects toward each other through empty space, as if they were connected by invisible ropes. In Einstein's model, space isn't empty, but is a material that is shaped by the mass of an object. In this model, objects fall toward each other because they are trapped in the bending of space caused by their masses.

At the same time, the planet or moon has a great deal of momentum that keeps it circling around the larger body, which keeps it from falling into the larger body, at least for a while. If a body has too much momentum, it may orbit the larger body a few times, and then escape the gravity well, continuing past the larger body. If the gravity and momentum match just right, however, the smaller body will enter a stable orbit around the larger body, circling it for a long time.

ESSENTIAL QUESTION

How are the two types of craters made?

What else is there to see in the vast stretches of space? Comets and asteroids! We'll take a closer look at these hurling balls of frozen water and gas in the next chapter.

CRATER MAKER

Craters come in different sizes and shapes. Make models of impact craters and volcanic craters to better understand how they form.

Caution: Do not fire anything from your slingshot at a person or animal or anything breakable. Wear protective eyewear in this experiment.

❯ **What do you think affects the size and shape of craters?** Write down your hypothesis in your science journal.

❯ **Cut a small hole in the side of a box lid, big enough to slide in a straw.** Push a straw through the hole with the bendy end on the outside of the box lid. Bend the end of the straw so it points up. Crimp the end of another straw and slide it into the end of the first straw inside the box lid. Bend the end of the second straw so that it points upward inside the lid. Tape the straws where they join down to the bottom of the lid.

❯ **Fill the lid with sand or dirt almost to the top.** Cover the end of the straw inside. Put a thin layer of a different color sand or dirt on top of the first one.

❯ **To make a volcanic crater, take a deep breath and quickly expel the air through the straw.** Your breath  represents the exploding gas, hot magma, and ash escaping from under the surface of the planet. Write down your observations in your science journal.

❯ **To make an impact crater, find a place with soft soil or sand outside.** Make a slingshot by tying rubber bands to the ends of a forked stick.

❯ **Place a pebble in the middle of the rubber band of your slingshot.** Aim your slingshot toward a patch of dirt or sand. Gently pull the rubber band back and then release it. You could also drop the pebbles into your box without the slingshot.

> **Use a ruler to measure the depth and width of each crater.** Write down your observations in your science journal. You can also put your results into a chart. Compare your results to your hypothesis.

Try This!

How will changing the size of pebbles change your results? Write down your prediction in your science journal and then test your ideas. What happens if you drop the pebbles from different heights or angles? Look for differences in crater size and shape. Do the impact craters overlap? Write down your observations in your science journal. You could also try making impact craters in wet sand. How does this change your results?

Meteorites

Meteoroids are small particles of space dust and rock that orbit the sun. They can fall into the earth's atmosphere where they burn up, becoming meteors. If part of the rock lands on Earth, it is called a **meteorite**. Have you ever seen a shooting star? This was actually a meteor burning up in the earth's atmosphere. If you're lucky and you plan well, you might get to see a meteor shower. These are times when Earth is passing through a trail of dusty debris left behind by a passing comet. On these nights, which happen regularly during the year, you might see anywhere from 50 to 100 shooting stars per hour. Meteor showers are usually named after a star or **constellation** that is in the same area of the sky as the shooting stars. One of the most famous meteor showers is called the Perseids. These happen in mid-August every year, and are a result of the comet called Swift-Tuttle, which leaves a cloud of debris when it swings by the sun every 135 years.

WORDS TO KNOW

meteoroid: a piece of dust or rock orbiting around the sun.

meteorite: a piece of rock that falls from space and lands on Earth's surface.

constellation: a group of stars that form a shape or pattern. There are 88 official constellations in the sky.

THE MOON ORBITS THE EARTH

This activity will help you understand how the moon orbits around the earth.

❯ **Cut a black plastic trash bag so you have one large sheet of plastic.** Pinch the center of the bag and tie a rubber band around it. Fill a small plastic bottle with water or sand and tie it around the pinched center of the bag. Place the bottle in the center of a large cardboard box.

❯ **Pull the plastic sheet around the edges of the cardboard box.** Pull it tight so that the bottle pulls the center of the sheet down into the center. This plastic sheet represents the fabric of space and time and the center is the gravity well created by the mass of the earth.

❯ **Place a globe in the center of the plastic sheet, in its gravity well.** Tape a 1-foot-long stick to the top of the globe. Wrap a few layers of tape around the top of the stick, half an inch or so down from the top.

❯ **Tie a loose loop in one end of a piece of string and place it around the stick, resting on top of the tape.** It should be loose enough to rotate easily around the stick, but not enough to slide down past the tape. Attach the other end of the string to a small ball, leaving enough length for the ball to roll along inside the gravity well.

❯ **Swing the moon to the left around the earth.** How many times can you get it to orbit the earth? Record your observations in your science journal.

Think More

Why does your moon orbit only a few times? Write down your ideas in your science journal.

Chapter 4

BEYOND PLANETS AND
STARS

There's more to the solar system than planets, stars, and moons. There are comets, asteroids, dwarf planets, and even different kinds of stars. In fact, astronomers are discovering new celestial objects out there all the time.

For example, no one knew about the **Kuiper Belt** until 1992, though Pluto, one of the residents of the Kuiper Belt, had been spotted in 1930. It took astronomers David Jewitt (1958–) and Jane Luu (1963–) aiming a massive telescope from on top of Mauna Kea in Hawaii to begin finding more Pluto-like objects in the region. Some of these celestial objects are big enough to be considered **dwarf planets**.

ESSENTIAL QUESTION

Why do some celestial objects remain undiscovered for so many centuries?

51

WORDS TO KNOW

Kuiper Belt: a large belt of comets and asteroids that orbits the sun in an area at about 100 AU.

dwarf planet: similar to a planet but not massive enough to clear its orbit of other, similar objects.

classify: to put things in groups based on what they have in common.

DWARF PLANETS

A dwarf planet is big enough to have been pulled into a round shape by its own gravity. It orbits the sun, rather than orbiting another planet as a moon does. However, unlike the eight planets in our solar system, a dwarf planet is not large enough to clear objects out of its orbit.

In 2003, a team of astronomers in California, led by Mike Brown (1965–), discovered a celestial body bigger than Pluto. This object caused a lot of disagreement among astronomers. Some thought this should be a 10th planet. Others did not think it qualified to be a planet. But, if this object was not a planet, should Pluto be called a planet?

Pluto

credit: NASA/Johns Hopkins University Applied Physics Laboratory/Southwest Research Institute/Alex Parker

Finding New Planets

In 1781, William Herschel (1738–1822), a British astronomer, discovered a new planet, Uranus. He originally named it George's Planet, after King George III (1738–1820) of England. In keeping with the tradition of other planets being named after Greek and Roman gods, astronomers eventually named the planet Uranus after the Greek god of the sky. Astronomers then noticed irregularities in the orbit of Uranus. The irregularities suggested that the gravitational pull of another planet beyond Uranus was slowing Uranus down. In 1846, Johann Galle (1812–1910), using data from Urbain Le Verrier (1811–1877), discovered the planet. It was named Neptune for the Roman god of the sea. In 1930, Clyde Tombaugh (1906–1997) discovered an object 39 times farther from the sun than the earth. The object was Pluto—named after the Roman god of the underworld.

All this disagreement led to a new classification—dwarf planet.

In 2006, Pluto went from being the ninth planet in the solar system to being classified a dwarf planet. The asteroid Ceres was also reclassified as a dwarf planet. Because of all the disagreement it caused among astronomers, the new object was appropriately named Eris, after the Greek goddess of discord. A day on Eris is about two hours longer than a day on Earth. And it takes Eris 557 Earth years to make one revolution around the sun.

DID YOU KNOW?

Astronomer Clyde Tombaugh, who discovered Pluto, died in 1997. He wanted his ashes to be sent into space. In 2015, the *New Horizons* spacecraft flew past Pluto with his ashes onboard.

PS There are dwarf planets in the Kuiper Belt that have thin atmospheres. What happens to the atmospheres when the planets move away from the sun? Why do you think this is? **Read more about the Kuiper Belt at this website.**

🔍 NASA Kuiper

Since then, scientists have discovered more dwarf planets. Our solar system may have hundreds more dwarf planets—scientists don't know how many.

KUIPER BELT

Past Neptune, the solar system gets relatively crowded in the Kuiper Belt, which extends as far as 100 AU. The Kuiper Belt contains hundreds of thousands of icy objects. These objects are called **Kuiper Belt Objects (KBOs)**. Some scientists suggest that there may be 100 million objects more than half a mile wide in the belt. The first object to be seen in the Kuiper Belt was Pluto in 1930. Pluto is relatively close to the sun compared to other KBOs. Pluto's orbit is more elliptical than the other planets, so it sometimes comes closer to the sun than Neptune.

Pluto also has three moons, named Charon, Nix, and Hydra, after characters in Greek mythology.

So far, the farthest known observable object from the sun that is still part of the solar system is an object named V774104. Astronomers discovered the object in 2015.

New Horizons

In 2006, NASA launched the *New Horizons* spacecraft. Nine years later, it became the first spacecraft to explore Pluto and the Kuiper Belt. By exploring Pluto, scientists hoped to learn more about what the solar system looked like when it formed more than 4 billion years ago. *New Horizons* made many exciting discoveries. It sent images back to Earth of spiky ice structures on the surface of Pluto. Some of them were as high as skyscrapers! One of the most important discoveries was images of what looked like ice, flowing on the planet's surface. As of 2018, *New Horizons* is still exploring space. NASA is using the spacecraft to investigate more icy worlds in the Kuiper Belt. No one knows what the spacecraft will discover next.

An artist's drawing of the Kuiper Belt, with Pluto's orbit in yellow
credit: NASA

V774104 is 100 times farther from the sun than Earth. Scientists believe that it could be up to 600 miles across. Objects such as V774104, which orbits the sun past Neptune, are called trans-Neptunian objects, or TNOs.

Scientists created a video based on data from the *New Horizons* spacecraft of the surface of Pluto.

What do you notice about the surface of the dwarf planet?

PS

🔍 NASA New Horizons Pluto

PULSARS

In 1967, astronomer Jocelyn Bell (1943–) discovered the first **pulsar** while working with Professor Antony Hewish (1924–) at Glasgow University. A pulsar is a kind of **neutron star** that pulses as it spins incredibly fast. Some pulsars spin thousands of times a minute! The fastest known pulsar was discovered in 2017. Known as J0952, this pulsar rotates 707 times a second!

WORDS TO KNOW

astrophysicist: a person who studies what makes up the stars and universe.

radio astronomy: a branch of astronomy that uses giant radio antennas to detect radiation emitted from astronomical objects.

radiation: the process by which energy such as light or sound moves from its source and radiates outward.

methane: a colorless, odorless gas that burns easily.

Neutron stars are the densest stars that astronomers know of. They form when a huge star called a supernova explodes. The iron in the core of the supernova squeezes together until all its protons and electrons change into neutrons.

The resulting neutron star, as its name suggests, is made almost completely of neutrons.

DID YOU KNOW?

When Jocelyn Bell Burnell and Antony Hewish first discovered pulsars, they jokingly called them LGM. The acronym stood for Little Green Men. The radio signal from the star was so regular that it looked like a signal from aliens!

As the neutron star rotates on its axis, it produces pulses of electromagnetic energy, including radio waves. This energy sweeps across the sky, shining on one part of the sky before moving on like the spinning beacon in a lighthouse.

Jocelyn Bell Burnell

Jocelyn Bell Burnell (1943–) is an **astrophysicist** from Northern Ireland. She was the first person to discover a pulsar, in 1967, while she was a graduate student at the University of Cambridge. She discovered it with her teacher, Antony Hewish (1924–), using a radio telescope that he had designed. Antony later received the Nobel Prize for this discovery. Many people thought that Jocelyn should have shared the prize, though Jocelyn did not hold that view. In 2018, Jocelyn received the Special Breakthrough Prize in Fundamental Physics, which came with a cash award of more than $2 million, all of which she donated to help women, ethnic minorities, and refugee students become physics researchers.

COMETS

Have you ever seen a comet hovering in the sky? That streak of light might not look like it's moving very fast, but in fact, that comet could be traveling between 6 and 43 miles per second!

Comets are frozen chunks of water, **methane**, and ice mixed in with dirt and dust. They are often compared to dirty snowballs. And even if you don't see them every night when you look up to the sky, there are billions or even trillions of comets in a region on the edges of our solar system called the Oort Cloud.

DID YOU KNOW?

The Oort Cloud is named after astronomer Jan Oort (1900–1992). He was a pioneer in the use of **radio astronomy**, which uses giant radio antennas to detect the **radiation** emitted from celestial objects that scientists use to learn more about the objects.

Comet NEAT
credit: NASA

WORDS TO KNOW

long-period comet: a comet with an orbit longer than 200 years.

short-period comet: a comet with an orbit shorter than 200 years.

solar wind: the stream of electrically charged particles emitted by the sun.

Scientists believe that the Oort Cloud is like an icy bubble. It may reach from our sun to the next star—a distance of up to 100,000 AU. The Oort Cloud is believed to be the source of **long-period comets**. These are comets that can take more than a thousand years to travel around the sun. Some may even take 30 million years to make this journey!

Direct study has not yet proved the Oort Cloud exists, but most scientists believe that it does. In 1977, NASA launched the unmanned space probe *Voyager 1* to study the outer solar system. In 2013, *Voyager 1* left our solar system, becoming the first object made by humans to do so. The probe, however, will not reach the Oort Cloud for another 300 years. Does it seem strange to launch a project that no one alive now will see the conclusion of?

DID YOU KNOW?

On May 1, 1996, NASA's *Ulysses* spacecraft crossed the tail of the Comet Hyakutake. Using data from the spacecraft, scientists made an incredible discovery. The comet's tail was more than 354 million miles long! The tail of Comet Hyakutake is the longest ever measured.

Short-period comets come from an area inside Neptune's orbit called the Kuiper Belt. Many scientists believe that these comets formed there. Short-period comets usually complete their orbits in less than 200 years.

Halley's Comet is an example of a short-period comet. The comet was named for eighteenth-century astronomer Edmond Halley (1656–1742). From Earth, Halley's Comet is visible once every 74 to 79 years. The comet last visited Earth in 1986, so it is not expected to return until 2061. Maybe you'll see it then!

Astronomers theorize that some comets get bumped out of the Kuiper Belt or the Oort Cloud by the gravitational pushing and pulling of other comets. The bumped comets then fall into orbits that take them closer to the sun and the earth. When they get closer to the sun, these comets begin to heat up. The heat causes the ice in the comets to vaporize. The **solar wind** then blows the gas and dust away from the sun. From Earth, the gas and dust look like two long tails. Comet tails can stretch for more than millions of miles!

Predicting the Future

In the past, some people believed that comets could predict the future. People usually believed that comets were a sign of bad things to come, such as wars or natural disasters. In 1910, the approach of Halley's Comet caused widespread panic. In North America, newspapers reported that the comet's tail contained a deadly poison. People began sealing their windows and doors. Some people purchased gas masks. Crooks sold comet pills they claimed would keep people safe from the effects of the poison. The pills were worthless. Most contained sugar, but the public didn't believe this. When the comet passed by Earth, nothing happened, and people realized how foolish they had been. There is no reason to be frightened of a comet.

You can read original news articles about the Halley's Comet panic at this website. Is there anything today that makes people concerned like this?

🔍 Hubble comet history

WORDS TO KNOW

speculate: to make a guess or theory about something without having all the information.

sphere: a three-dimensional round shape, like a ball.

accretion: the process of particles sticking together to form larger objects, such as asteroids or planets.

ASTEROID BELT

Between Mars and Jupiter lies an area known as the asteroid belt. This region is home to millions of asteroids, which are small, rocky objects that orbit the sun. In movies, the asteroids look as if they are close together and people in spaceships have to duck and dodge them. But if you were to stand on one of these asteroids, you probably wouldn't be able to see another one. The asteroids in the belt are spaced far apart—an average of 600,000 miles.

Astronomers used to **speculate** that the asteroid belt was the remains of an early planet that was ripped apart by the gravitational pull of Jupiter.

Now, most suspect that the gravity of Jupiter kept a planet from ever forming from all those rocky objects.

Asteroids come in dozens of irregular shapes. Some asteroids look like peanuts, lumpy potatoes, and cigars. One unusual asteroid called Kleopatra looks like a dog bone! Asteroids are not round like planets because their gravity is usually too weak for them to pull themselves into **spheres**.

DID YOU KNOW?

The word *asteroid* means "star-like" in Greek. When astronomers first saw the tiny points of light of asteroids, the light reminded them of stars. Now, scientists know that asteroids are not stars, but the name stuck. Stars such as our sun produce light and energy. Asteroids do not produce light—their surfaces reflect the sun's light. What other celestial object does this?

An artist's drawing of an asteroid belt
credit: NASA/JPL-Caltech

Scientists believe that asteroids, like planets, formed through a process called **accretion**. As millions of years passed, dust and rocks spun around and around in space. The dust and small rocks collided with each other, forming larger rocks. How did the rocks stick together? Gravity held them together. Some rocks grew so large that they formed planets. Other rocks never grew large enough to form planets.

Asteroids could have formed through thousands of these collisions. The craters on the surfaces of asteroids provide evidence of these collisions.

credit: NASA/JPL-Caltech/UCLA/MPS/DLR/IDA

CERES

Ceres is the largest asteroid in the asteroid belt. Italian priest and amateur astronomer Giuseppe Piazzi (1746–1826) spotted Ceres in 1801. He named the asteroid after the Roman goddess of harvests, Ceres. In 2006, scientists decided that Ceres was a dwarf planet.

In 2015, NASA's *Dawn* spacecraft reached the orbit of Ceres. No spacecraft had ever visited a dwarf planet before. Data from the spacecraft showed that the surface of Ceres continues to change.

Find out more about the *Dawn* mission and Ceres.

PS

🔍 Dawn mission

Images from *Dawn* showed that the amount of ice on one of the asteroid's craters increases as Ceres's orbit takes it closer to the sun.

All of the objects in space are fascinating, but how do we know about things that are so far away from us? We've mentioned different spacecraft and instruments that scientists have sent into space to collect data—in the next chapter, we'll take a closer look at some of the technology that makes it possible for us to get a glimpse of worlds beyond our own.

ESSENTIAL QUESTION

Why do some celestial objects remain undiscovered for so many centuries?

SOLAR WIND MODEL

When the solar wind hits a comet, something exciting happens. The particles knock off some bits of ice and dust from the comet that stream out behind the comet as it flies along, like a tail. Sunlight then reflects off the tail, making it visible to us. In this activity, you can model this effect. You'll be using dry ice, which you can get at some grocery stores.

Caution: Have an adult help you handle the dry ice!

❯ **Place an electric fan and a saucer or other shallow container on a table or counter in a dark room.** Position them so that the fan is blowing across the top of the saucer. The fan will represent the solar wind.

❯ **Use heavy gloves or tongs to put the dry ice in the saucer. Important:** Never touch dry ice directly with your skin. It can cause severe frostbite that feels like being burned.

❯ **Pour some water on the dry ice and into the saucer.** Turn on the fan. Turn out the lights in the room and turn on the flashlight. Aim the flashlight directly at the dry ice and the tail of vapor that is flowing out behind it. Write down your observations in your science journal and add diagrams.

Think More

A comet's tail always points away from the sun. This means that the tail can be in front or behind the comet. Look at your notes and answer the following questions. Is the comet's tail in front or behind as it moves away from the sun? What do you notice about the comet's tail when the comet is closer to the sun?

DID YOU KNOW?

When the solar wind hits the earth's magnetic field near the North or South Poles, the electrically charged particles react with the magnetic field, giving off waves of light called the aurora borealis, or northern lights, and the aurora australis, or southern lights. These are best seen near the earth's poles, where the magnetic field is the strongest.

MAKE YOUR OWN PULSAR MODEL

When a pulsar shines, the light looks like it is turning off and on because the pulsar is rotating. This activity helps you to explore a pulsar's pulse.

❯ **Place a pencil through the center of a CD.** Use clay to hold the pencil in place. You are making a device like a spinning top.

❯ **Tape a small flashlight across the CD, perpendicular to the pencil.** Most pulsars have their magnetic poles and rotational axis closer together. But this model will still give you an idea of how pulsars work.

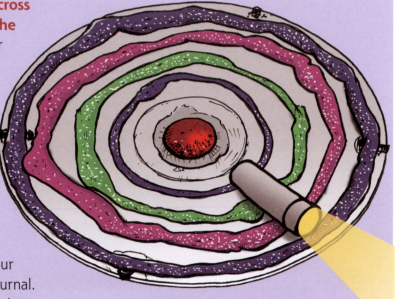

❯ **Turn on the flashlight and turn off the lights.** Spin the top on the floor. Focus your sight at the flashlight as it shines at you. Afterward, write down your observations in your science journal. When the light is pointed directly at you, does it appear to blink on and off like a pulsar? Because you are in a room, you should see the light bouncing off the walls. But in outer space, there is very little for the beam to bounce off, so it looks like the pulsar is winking only at you!

WORDS TO KNOW

perpendicular: when an object forms a right angle with another object.

Try This!

Repeat this experiment outside at night. Will your results be the same or different? Write a prediction in your science journal. Record your observations in your science journal and compare them with your prediction.

Crab Nebula

In 1054 CE, astronomers in China witnessed a bright light in the sky. The light was a supernova explosion 6,500 light-years from Earth. The remains of this supernova are called the Crab Nebula. The nebula is massive. Today, it is approximately 12 light-years across! In the center of the nebula is the Crab pulsar. The pulsar spins around 33 times each second.

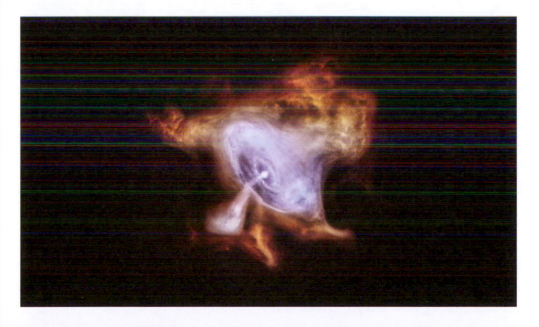

 View some more images from NASA of the Crab Nebula.

🔎 YouTube Crab Nebula NASA

Chapter 5

FROM ANCIENT ASTRONOMY TO
TELESCOPES

How do we know about the solar system? People have studied the solar system for thousands of years. The earliest astronomical tools were our eyes. Many ancient civilizations, including the Mesopotamians in the Middle East and the Maya in Central America, studied the night sky.

The land of the Mesopotamians was between the Tigris and Euphrates Rivers in what is now Iraq. Astronomers in Mesopotamia kept records of the stars and planets for hundreds of years. They recorded their observations on stone tablets. The tablets were accurate because these ancient astronomers used advanced **geometry** to track the movements of the planets. The scientists used their observations to plan festivals and other important events in the Mesopotamian calendar and to make predictions.

ESSENTIAL QUESTION

How did the telescope change astronomers' views of the solar system?

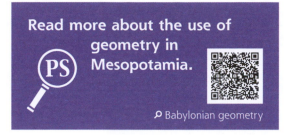

Read more about the use of geometry in Mesopotamia.

🔍 Babylonian geometry

WORDS TO KNOW

geometry: a branch of mathematics that deals with points, lines, and shapes and where they are in space.

observatory: a place from which astronomers can observe the planets, stars, and galaxies.

Two thousand years ago, the Maya people lived in an area that stretched from southern Mexico to Central America. Around 200 CE, the Maya began to build cities with palaces, temples, and **observatories**. The most famous of these observatories is El Caracol in Chichen Itza. You can still see the observatory.

From observatories such as El Caracol, the Maya studied the sun, moon, planets, and stars. The ancient Maya learned to predict eclipses. They were able to correctly note the movements of Venus. They also used their observations of the sky and mathematics to create calendars. Mayan astronomers created one calendar based on the movements of the sun.

The ruins of El Caracol in Chichen Itza

credit: Metal Island (public domain)

Learn more about Maya calendar systems here. How are they similar to the calendar we use today?

Smithsonian Mayan calendar

EARLY TELESCOPES

In the early 1600s, Italian scientist Galileo Galilei heard about a new Dutch invention, the spy glass, or telescope. People in Europe were using the spy glass to make objects appear larger. This was a particularly useful tool when looking for sailing ships coming over the horizon.

In 1608, a Dutch lens maker named Hans Lippershey (1570–1619) tried to **patent** his spy glass design, but it was not approved. Galileo set out to improve upon the design. During the course of several years, Galileo experimented with lenses. Through trial and error, he figured out what sizes the lenses should be and how far apart he should space them. His telescope used a **convex** lens at the end of a hollow tube to gather and bend the light. A second eyepiece lens was smaller and **concave**. This type of telescope is called a **refracting telescope**. Lenses in refracting telescopes bend light.

Galileo was also able to make lenses so powerful that they could magnify objects up to 30 times. In 1610, Galileo placed his lenses in a hollow tube and aimed it at the night sky.

A replica of a Galilean telescope

Watch a video about Galileo's telescope here.
What's the difference between an inventor and an innovator?

🔎 Galileo telescope innovator

Galileo discovered that the planets were not stars—they were worlds like Earth. He saw that Saturn had rings, the sun had sunspots, and the moon had craters. Galileo also observed four dots of light surrounding Jupiter. He first thought that the four objects were stars, but later correctly guessed that they were moons orbiting Jupiter.

Galileo's observations were the first proof that not everything in the universe revolved around the earth.

Galileo's Acceleration Ramp

In addition to studying the night sky, Galileo studied the speed of falling objects. In Galileo's day, people believed that a moving object would eventually come to a stop. Galileo's experiments showed that a moving object would keep on rolling if no friction slowed it down. In one experiment, he rolled bronze balls down a wooden board on a slope and up another. He noticed that the balls sped up, even without anyone pushing them, and that the greater the angle of the ramp, the faster the balls **accelerated**, or sped up. Galileo was able to show that the rate at which the balls sped up was the same. It didn't matter how big or heavy the balls were, they all accelerated at the same rate. Another scientist, Sir Isaac Newton, later realized that the force that Galileo had measured in timing falling objects was the same force that caused the planets to orbit around the sun and the moon to orbit the earth—gravity! This was one of the greatest scientific insights of all time. One story claims that Newton figured this out when he saw an apple fall from a tree, while the moon hung in the sky behind the tree. People thought it made a better story to say that the apple hit him on the head.

Check out this video on Isaac Newton and gravity.
Why was this such a revolutionary discovery?

🔎 CrashCourse Newtonian physics

WORDS TO KNOW

geocentric: the belief, now disproved, that the earth is the center of the solar system.

retrograde rotation: rotating in the opposite direction of normal.

heliocentric: the belief that the sun is the center of the solar system.

BCE: put after a date, BCE stands for Before Common Era and counts down to zero. CE stands for Common Era and counts up from zero. These non-religious terms correspond to BC and AD. This book was printed in 2019 CE.

THE HELIOCENTRIC AND GEOCENTRIC DEBATE

Have you ever seen the earth move? It's hard to see, because you're standing on the earth as it moves. Have you seen the sun move? It sure looks like the sun is moving as it rises in the east in the morning and sets in the west in the evening. For thousands of years, people believed that the earth was the center of the universe and the sun moved around the earth. This is the **geocentric** theory of the solar system.

While to ancient astronomers, the sun, the moon, and the planets appeared to travel around Earth, the geocentric theory did not explain the motion of the planets.

When these astronomers studied the sky, they noticed that the planets looked like they were moving backward in their orbits. This movement is called **retrograde rotation**.

The Egyptian astronomer Ptolemy (c. 100–170) accounted for this retrograde motion by suggesting that the planets were mounted on invisible, crystal spheres. The spheres spun as the planets revolved around the earth. Ptolemy explained that when the planets appeared to move backward, they were in fact rotating away from Earth on their spheres.

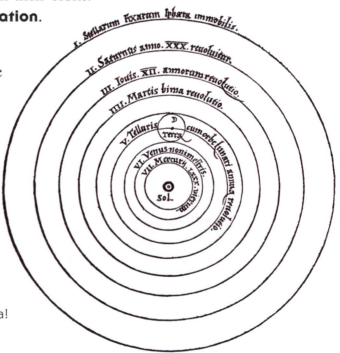

Nicolaus Copernicus's diagram of the solar system with the sun at the center. A revolutionary idea!

Ptolemy could then predict where the planets would be. His prediction was based on the speed at which the spheres rotated, and the speed at which they revolved around the earth.

In the sixteenth century, a Polish astronomer had a new and exciting idea to explain the movement of the planets. In his 1543 book, *On the Revolution of Heavenly Bodies*, Nicolaus Copernicus (1473–1543) explained that the earth and the other planets moved around the sun. This is the **heliocentric** model of the solar system. Much earlier, a Greek astronomer, Aristarchus (c. 310–230 **BCE**), had also suggested that the earth rotated around the sun. But his ideas had been quickly forgotten. Copernicus also encountered difficulty in having his ideas accepted.

The Roman Catholic Church banned his book for 75 years. Why are people sometimes reluctant to accept new scientific theories?

It wasn't until the 1600s that astronomers again began to question the idea of the earth being the center of the universe. In 1609, German astronomer Johannes Kepler (1571–1630) published his ideas on the movement of the planets in *Astronomia Nova (The New Astronomy)*. Kepler used his own observations and those of his mentor, Tycho Brahe (1546–1601), to improve upon the Copernicus model. Kepler believed that the planets did not revolve around the sun in perfect circles. Instead, the planets revolved in elliptical orbits around the sun. Ellipses explain the apparent retrograde motion of the other planets.

During the seventeenth century, there were three models of the universe. Each model explained the movement of the planets, then called "wandering stars." Why did these models become less accurate through time? **You can learn more about these models and Johannes Kepler here.**

PS

Kepler's discovery

WORDS TO KNOW

parallax: the apparent change in position of a star compared to the stars behind it, as viewed from one side of the earth's orbit around the sun and compared to the view from the other side, half a year later.

radio wave: an electromagnetic wave used for sending radio or television signals through the air.

It took more than 200 years for scientists to confirm that the earth orbits the sun. This is when Friedrich Bessel (1784–1846), a German mathematician and astronomer, became the first person to measure the distance to a star. He used what's called stellar **parallax**.

The Greek scientist Aristotle (384–322 BCE) had reasoned that if the earth moves around the sun, the stars would look different from one side of the sun to the other. For example, hold your arm out in front of you with your thumb out. Close one eye and look at an object in the distance, such as a tree. Move your head to the right. Your thumb (the closer star) will look as if it is to the left of the tree (a distant star). Move your head to the left, and your thumb will appear to move to the right. Your thumb is not moving, however—your eye (the earth) is moving. Aristotle could not see any parallax, so he assumed that Earth was not moving.

The problem was that the distances from Earth to the stars were so great—compared to the distance the earth moves around the sun—that the parallax could not be observed with the naked eye.

In 1838, Bessel succeeded in measuring the parallax of star 61 Cygni using an advanced telescope and geometry. The star, sometimes called Bessel's Star, is about 11 light-years, or 60 trillion miles, away from Earth.

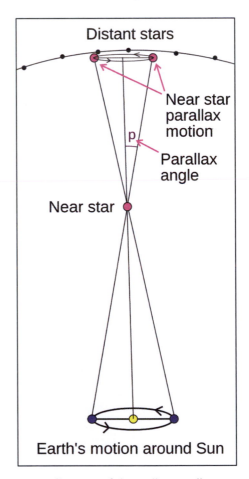

Distant stars

Near star parallax motion

p

Parallax angle

Near star

Earth's motion around Sun

A diagram of the stellar parallax

MODERN TELESCOPES

Telescopes have come a long way since Galileo. The world's largest telescope is located on the peak of a volcano in the Canary Islands in Spain! Its mirror is 34 feet across and made of 36 hexagonal pieces that can be removed, altered, and replaced. This telescope took seven years to build—weather conditions and the remote location made the process a difficult one. Finally, in 2009, scientists could begin using it to record data.

Another important telescope here on land is the Atacama Large Millimeter Array in the Atacama Desert of northern Chile. This telescope is one of the highest, permanent, ground-based telescopes in the world.

You might wonder how astronomers use these telescopes. They aren't looking through an eyepiece and sweeping the skies with their own vision! Instead, a bank of powerful satellites collects all kinds of data, such as **radio waves**, which is then processed by computers that can look for patterns and irregularities.

The Atacama Large Millimeter Array in Chile
credit: ESO/C. Malin (CC BY 4.0)

NEW TOOLS

Some of the best new tools for learning about the solar system are space telescopes. Telescopes on Earth do not allow astronomers to clearly focus on objects. When light passes through Earth's atmosphere, it becomes **distorted**. Imagine looking at an object through a glass of water. Dust, air pollution, clouds, water vapor, and air currents interfere with the light. Those distant space objects then appear blurry. But space telescopes allow astronomers on Earth to focus clearly on distant objects.

An image of the planetary nebula NGC 2818 taken by the Hubble Space Telescope, 2008

credit: NASA, ESA, and the Hubble Heritage Team (STScI/AURA)

How do telescopes analyze color? **Learn about the information that can be found in wavelengths in this video.**

🔍 NASA black hole Webb

On April 24, 1990, NASA launched the first space-based telescope, the Hubble Space Telescope, into orbit above Earth. Almost the size of a school bus, the Hubble piggybacked its way into space on a space shuttle. Astronomers have been using the Hubble to look at some of the earliest galaxies in the universe.

The Hubble has made more than a million observations and taken pictures of stars, planets, and galaxies.

DID YOU KNOW?

The James Webb Space Telescope will be as large as a tennis court!

Soon, scientists will have another amazing tool to explore the universe with. It is the James Webb Space Telescope, or Webb. Planned for nearly 20 years, the Webb is the most powerful and largest telescope ever constructed for space. The current launch date is set for March 2021. Astronomers will be able to use the Webb to study the earliest galaxies.

People have been gazing upward and studying the solar system from the comfort of our planet for centuries, but it was only recently that we were able to take a closer look at other planets, comets, asteroids, and much more. We'll learn about satellites, rovers, and probes—and how they are able to travel so far—in the next chapter.

ESSENTIAL QUESTION

How did the telescope change astronomers' views of the solar system?

NEWTONIAN TELESCOPE

Ideas for supplies: cardboard box, scissors, large plastic bowl, clay or plaster, sandpaper, glue, aluminum foil or silver Mylar from a balloon, small mirror, tape, several long sticks, science journal, and pencil

In this activity, you will build a Newtonian telescope. A Newtonian telescope uses mirrors instead of lenses to gather light. Sir Isaac Newton created his reflecting telescope in 1668.

❯ **Open up the cardboard box.** Carefully use scissors to remove one whole side of it.

❯ **You need a large plastic bowl that will fit in the bottom of the box.** Fill it with clay or plaster and let it dry. Use sandpaper to smooth the plaster into a smooth, concave surface.

❯ **Cover the surface of the plaster with a thin coat of glue, and then with aluminum foil or mylar.** Be very careful to smooth out any wrinkles in the surface. This makes your reflector.

❯ **Position the bowl at the closed end of the cardboard box, with the concave surface facing the open end of the box.** Tape it securely in place.

❯ **Mount the small mirror on a stick.** Place it in the middle of the box, about 10 inches from the bowl, at a 45-degree angle. Use tape to secure the mirror in place.

❯ **Cut a small hole in the side of the box next to the small mirror.** Position the hole so that the light gathered by the reflector bounces off the mirror and through the hole.

❯ **Bring the box outside and brace it against a stable surface.** Point the open end at a bright object in the night sky, such as the moon, and look through the hole in the side of the box.

DID YOU KNOW?

The S.A.L.T. (South African Large Telescope) has a mirror more than 36 feet across.

Try This!

What you made is a very simple Newtonian telescope. You can make an even better quality one by grinding a glass reflector and having it silvered—covered with a reflective material. However, this requires specialized equipment, as well as adult assistance. If you are interested, check the resources section for some websites and books that can get you started.

GALILEAN TELESCOPE

In this activity, you will make a simple telescope. You will need lenses from an old pair of eyeglasses or magnifying glasses.

Caution: Never look directly at the sun.

▶ **Take one paper towel tube and cut it lengthwise, on one side only.** Curl one side of the cut edge over the other side, so that this tube slides snugly inside another paper towel tube. Hold it at this size, take it out of the second tube, and tape it along its edge, so it keeps that size. Place most of it inside the other tube.

▶ **Tape one lens to the outside of the larger end of your tubes.** If your lens is from eyeglasses, it will have a convex and a concave side. The middle of the convex side bends outward, while the concave side bends inward. Tape the lens so that the convex side faces the outside of the tube and the concave side faces the inside. This lens is called the objective lens.

▶ **Tape the other lens to the outside of the inner tube.** This is the eyepiece lens. Tape this lens with the convex side to the inside and the concave to the outside.

▶ **Looking through the smaller end of the telescope, aim your telescope at a faraway object.** Try moving the inner tube back and forth inside the larger one. What do you notice about the image? Does it move the image closer or farther away?

▶ **Aim your telescope at the moon.** What do you notice? Record your observations in your science journal. Add drawings to your notes.

Try This!

Try the same experiment with something closer, such as an object across the room. What do you notice about the object? Write your observations in your science journal.

Chapter 6

SENDING SPACECRAFT TO
SPACE

After the telescope, the next huge technological leap in astronomy was the development of rockets in the twentieth century. Rockets meant that scientists could get much closer to the objects in space—even close enough to step on, as Neil Armstrong and Buzz Aldrin did in 1969 when they landed on the moon.

A rocket works through **propulsion**. Gas is pushed out one end of the rocket, in the opposite direction to the one we want the rocket to go. This works because, as Isaac Newton discovered, for every action, there is an equal and opposite reaction.

ESSENTIAL QUESTION

Why can't spacecraft simply carry their fuel onboard?

WORDS TO KNOW

propulsion: pushing or moving an object forward.

Global Positioning System (GPS): a system of satellites, computers, and receivers that can determine the exact location of a receiver anywhere on the planet.

Rockets used for space exploration get their power from burning fuel. The earliest rockets, built by the Chinese 2,000 years ago, used gunpowder, while modern rockets use liquid oxygen and other fuels. The science of rocket fuel is always changing. And these rockets mean that we can send all kinds of tools into space where humans can't go.

PROBES

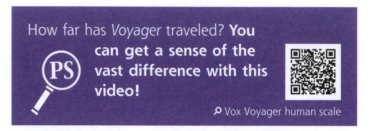

How far has *Voyager* traveled? **You can get a sense of the vast difference with this video!**

🔎 Vox Voyager human scale

In addition to space telescopes, spacecraft such as the Voyager and Galileo probes have visited the outer planets. The two Voyager probes were launched in 1977. They made many important discoveries, including finding active volcanoes on Io—Jupiter's moon—before heading out of the solar system. *Voyager 1* has gone the farthest from Earth of any human-made object.

Mars Research

Mars has been the subject of much astronomical research. The *Mariner 4* flew by Mars in 1964. Since then, the Soviet Mars and Phobos probes and NASA's Viking landers have all visited Mars, as have several more landers and orbiters, including the European Space Agency's *Mars Express Orbiter*. At the beginning of this century, six spacecraft were either in orbit around Mars or on its surface. The most successful of these have been the Mars exploration rovers—*Spirit* and *Opportunity*—which landed on Mars in 2004. Both NASA and the European Space Agency (ESA) have announced ambitious plans to send humans to Mars as early as 2024.

The *Galileo* probe traveled through the asteroid belt between Mars and Jupiter, and then circled Jupiter, studying its moons and atmosphere. It was deliberately crashed into Jupiter at the end of its mission to avoid an accidental crash landing into one of Jupiter's moons, which might have contaminated the moon with bacteria from Earth.

SATELLITES

Today, more than 1,300 active satellites are in orbit around Earth. A satellite is an object, like a moon, that orbits a planet. Some of these satellites are used for everyday activities such as broadcasting television signals and cell phone calls. Other satellites look for weather patterns on the earth. Some satellites communicate with **Global Positioning System (GPS)** devices, such as the navigation system your parents might have in their car. Yet other satellites contain scientific instruments, such as telescopes, for observing the stars and planets.

A replica of *Sputnik 1,* the very first artificial satellite
credit: NSSDC, NASA

WORDS TO KNOW

Soviet Union: a former country that included present-day Russia.

physics: the study of physical forces, including matter, energy, and motion, and how these forces interact with each other.

Space Race: the competition between the United States and the Soviet Union to achieve the greatest accomplishments in space exploration.

robotics: the science of designing, building, controlling, and operating robots.

Sputnik 1 was the world's first artificial satellite. The **Soviet Union** launched *Sputnik 1* into orbit around the earth on October 4, 1957. The launch was an important milestone in the history of exploration of the solar system. On January 31, 1958, the United States launched its first satellite, *Explorer 1*.

The first probe to land on another body in the solar system was the Soviet Union's *Luna 2* probe in 1959. It purposely crash-landed on the moon, and on the way there also discovered solar wind. The first mission to another planet was the U.S. *Mariner 2* mission, which passed near Venus in 1962. In 1966, the Soviet *Venera 3* probe was the first to enter Venus's atmosphere. These and later Venera and Mariner missions discovered much about the atmosphere and composition of Venus. The Venera and Mariner probes were all unmanned, however.

DID YOU KNOW?

The Chinese first built rockets more than 2,000 years ago. These used the same laws of **physics** as modern-day rockets.

During these years, the Soviet Union and United States competed to achieve the greatest accomplishments in space exploration. This was known as the "**Space Race**." The Space Race's greatest competition involved putting humans into space. Yuri Gagarin (1934–1968), a Soviet, was the first human in space in 1961, and his countrywoman, Valentina Tereshkova (1937–), became the first woman in space in 1963. In 1969, the first humans, Americans Neil Armstrong (1930–2012) and Buzz Aldrin (1930–), landed on the moon.

You can watch the *Apollo 11* moon landing video at this website. What must it have been like to be the first person to step on a celestial object that wasn't Earth?

PS

🔍 NASA Apollo 11

The American missions to the moon, called the Apollo missions, gathered much information about the moon, including samples of moon rocks that astronauts brought back to Earth.

More recent advances in computers, **robotics**, and remote-control technology mean that we can send much more complex probes into space without sending humans along. This saves a lot of energy because we don't have to send people and all the food and water they need to survive. Nor do we have to worry about getting them safely back to Earth.

Curiosity takes a selfie on Mars.
credit: NASA/JPL-Caltech/MSSS

spectrometer: an instrument used to study the properties of light.

gamma ray: light that has the shortest wavelength and highest energy.

ion: an atom with a positive or negative electrical charge. This means it has an extra electron or is missing an electron.

RED ROVER, RED ROVER

How do scientists explore the surface of Mars? Since 1997, NASA has landed robotic rovers on the surface of Mars. The first rover, *Sojourner*, landed in 1997. It was named for the African American abolitionist Sojourner Truth (c. 1797–1883). The rover was outfitted with equipment to take samples and photos of the terrain. Though *Sojourner* explored Mars for only 83 days, it paved the way for future missions.

Since this time, NASA has landed three more rovers on Mars—*Spirit*, *Opportunity*, and *Curiosity*. *Spirit* and *Opportunity* landed safely on Mars in 2004. Each rover investigated Mars with scientific instruments, including cameras, magnets for gathering magnetic dust, a rock abrasion tool for scratching rocks to see beneath their surfaces, a microscope, and **spectrometers**. Spectrometers are tools that analyze the light (or other kinds of electromagnetic radiation, such as **gamma rays**) given off by material to identify what it is made of.

The rovers also contained communication equipment. This equipment allowed controllers on Earth to steer the rovers and to upload new computer programs to the rovers' on-board computers.

Originally, *Spirit* and *Opportunity* were designed to last only three months on the Red Planet, as no humans would be there to repair them. But both rovers exceeded all expectations. *Spirit* explored Mars until May 25, 2011. *Opportunity* continued on the job until June 2018, when it went silent during a dust storm. After several months of trying to communicate with *Opportunity*, NASA decided, in February 2019, to say a final goodbye and officially end the mission. *Opportunity* had explored the Red Planet for more than 5,000 Martian days. The rover supplied scientists with valuable data, including evidence that Mars may have had liquid water on it at some time in the past.

This means it is possible that there was once life on Mars.

NASA's latest rover, *Curiosity*, landed on Mars on August 5, 2012. *Curiosity* has sent back nearly half a million images.

ION DRIVES

For decades, liquid- and solid-fuel rockets have been excellent for launching spacecraft into space. But as we want to travel farther and farther, we need better sources of energy to make that happen. The ion drive is one form of propulsion for long-range spaceflight. In 1998, NASA tested an ion propulsion system on the *Deep Space 1* spacecraft. The ESA's *SMART-1* satellite also used this technology on a mission to the moon's orbit in 2003. To understand the ion drive, you must know what an ion is: an atom that is electrically charged.

DID YOU KNOW?

NASA's *Dawn* spacecraft uses an **ion** engine to study the asteroid Vesta and the dwarf planet Ceres in the asteroid belt.

WORDS TO KNOW

nucleus: the central part of an atom, made up of protons and neutrons.

newton: a unit used to measure the amount of force you need to move something.

An atom is made up of a **nucleus** at the center and electrons around the nucleus. Electrons have a negative charge. The nucleus is made up of protons, which have a positive electrical charge, and neutrons, which have no charge.

If the number of electrons around a nucleus equals the number of protons within the nucleus, then the atom has a total charge of zero.

If, however, the number of electrons is greater than the number of protons, the atom will be negatively charged. And, if the number of electrons is less than the number of protons, the atom will be positively charged. Any atom with a charge, either positive or negative, is called an ion.

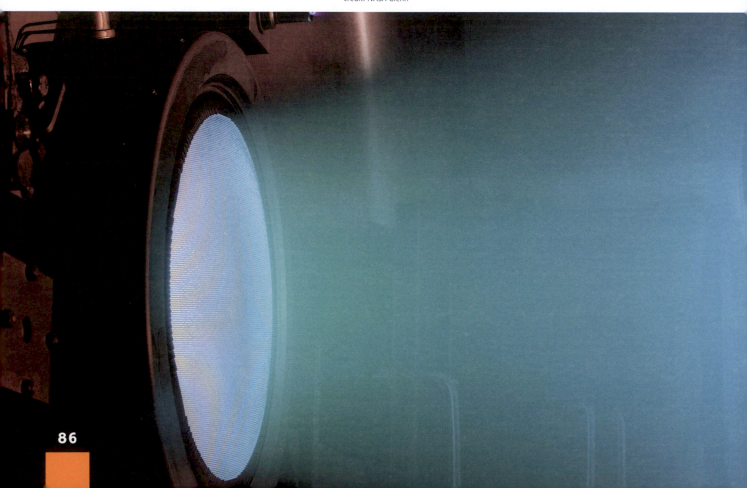

An ion drive being tested at NASA
credit: NASA Glenn

Have you ever used magnets and found that certain ends of the magnet won't meet, while other ends will click right together? That's a result of positive and negative magnetic fields coming into proximity with each other.

One of the laws of physics is that like charges (positive and positive, or negative and negative) repel each other, while unlike charges (positive and negative) attract each other.

So, if you have two negatively charged ions next to each other, they will be pushed apart by their electrical charges. This repulsion can be used to power a spaceship, through the ion drive.

An ion drive propels a spaceship forward by pushing ions out the back of the ship. The back of the ship will have a charge. And, when similarly charged ions are placed next to the charged section, these ions will shoot out the back, also pushing the ship forward. Remember, one of Newton's laws of motion says that for every action, there is an equal and opposite reaction. The initial push of the ion drive will be faint. But, as the drive continues, the speed will build up during a long time.

Ion Technology

Since 2016, more than 100 satellites have used ion thrusters to move in space. Engineers at NASA and the University of Michigan are busy developing new ion engines, including the NASA Evolutionary Xenon Thruster (X3). The X3 is already a record breaker. In tests conducted at the NASA Glenn Research Center in Ohio, the engine had a thrust of 5.4 **newtons** of force! The previous record was 3.3 newtons. In the future, ion technology such as the X3 could be used on a long-range mission to Mars. If the technology is successful, an ion engine could reduce the cost and duration of a mission to Mars.

BALLOONS

Balloons have long been used for exploring the earth and other planets in our solar system. Some balloons lift scientific instruments into the earth's atmosphere so we can learn more about the layers of gases that compose it. Studying the atmosphere helps scientists understand the weather. Weather balloons carry instruments high into the atmosphere, including thermometers to measure temperature and barometers to measure air pressure.

In 1984, the Soviet Space Agency launched balloon probes to lower instruments into the atmosphere of Venus as part of the Vega missions to Venus. A balloon used for taking such measurements is sometimes called an **aerostat** or an aerobot.

DID YOU KNOW?

In France in 1783, the Montgolfier brothers launched the first hot air balloon to carry humans.

Gravity Slingshots

Any spacecraft can benefit from the extra acceleration of a "gravity slingshot." When sending spacecraft to the far reaches of the solar system, we want to get them going as fast as possible because they have a long way to travel. The gravity slingshot works by sending a spacecraft to pass a planet. As the craft approaches the planet, the gravity of the planet pulls the craft toward it, speeding it up. Remember how the balls rolling down the gravity ramp sped up as they approached the bottom? The craft must be going fast enough, and not be aimed straight at the planet, so that the craft gains speed from passing by the planet but is not pulled into an orbit around the planet. In 2016, NASA's robotic *Juno* spacecraft used the gravity slingshot of Jupiter to increase its speed to 165,000 mph, making it the fastest spacecraft ever launched by humans.

A scientist launching a weather balloon. Balloons are used in many different aspects of earth and space science!

credit: NOAA's National Weather Service (NWS) Collection

Sending balloon aerostats on rockets to Venus helped scientists discover that the gases in its atmosphere trapped sunlight, creating a greenhouse effect. This makes Venus warmer than Mercury, even though Mercury is closer to the sun and receives more total sunlight. It is one of many examples of how studying other planets has helped us learn more about our own.

Each Vega balloon was roughly 10 feet wide with a gondola hanging 50 feet below it. The gondolas carried battery-powered instruments including barometers and thermometers. For almost two days, the Vega balloons floated in the atmosphere above Venus.

 Watch a video about the *Vega 2* balloon probe here.

🔍 YouTube Vega Venus balloon

89

SOLAR-POWERED SPACECRAFT

One of the problems in exploring the solar system is providing a power source for our rovers, satellites, and spacecraft. Not only do these machines have to get where they are going by rockets, ion drives, or other means, but they also need a power source for their cameras, sensors, computers, and communications equipment.

They could carry their power with them, either stored in batteries or as fuel for **generators**. However, that would be very heavy, requiring more energy to be lifted into space. And, eventually, the power would run out. Some exploratory craft get their power from small **nuclear power** generators. These require fuel, but a small amount of nuclear fuel can last a very long time.

Solar power is another power source. With solar power, you don't need to carry any fuel, as the sun is constantly shooting more sunlight out into the solar system. The Mars rovers, for example, have been powered by **solar cells**, which is one reason that their missions have lasted so long. The rovers have also been lucky that the winds on Mars periodically blow dust off their solar collectors, keeping them clear so they can keep receiving sunlight.

DID YOU KNOW?

The first solar-powered spacecraft was the *Vanguard 1*. NASA launched the 6-inch-wide spacecraft in 1958. *Vanguard 1* is no longer working, but it is the oldest artificial satellite orbiting Earth.

The largest solar-powered spacecraft is the *International Space Station* (*ISS*), which orbits the earth with a crew of astronauts and scientists. Each of the station's solar panel arrays is more than 100 feet long and almost 40 feet wide. **Want to see what the view looks like from the *ISS*? Check out this website!**

🔍 NASA HDEV ISS

Shake It Up, Baby!

A **seismometer** is one of the tools that we use to understand our planet, and to learn more about other planets. A seismometer measures movements of the earth's surface. Earth is seismically active—the movement of the tectonic plates over the molten mantle can cause earthquakes and volcanoes.

The Apollo astronauts placed seismometers on the surface of the moon. NASA **engineers** also included seismometers on probes that landed on Mars. In April 2018, NASA launched the Mars *InSight* (*Interior Exploration using Seismic Investigations*) lander. The lander will use **seismic** instruments and other advanced tools so that scientists back on Earth can learn more about the interior structure and composition of Mars.

Using solar power becomes more difficult the farther one gets from the sun, as less sunlight is available. For example, Mars receives only half of the sunlight of Earth, and the dwarf planet Ceres gets only about 10 percent. Because of this, most solar-powered spacecraft have been designed to be used near Earth or Mars. But improvements in the efficiency of solar cells have made it possible for space probes such as the *Juno* spacecraft to orbit Jupiter with solar power.

In the future, people on Earth could possibly get their power from giant, solar-powered satellites that would collect energy and beam it down to antennas. However, we would first need to create a cheap way—such as a space elevator—to get the materials to build these satellites in space!

ESSENTIAL QUESTION

Why can't spacecraft simply carry their fuel onboard?

As you can see, getting to space and moving in space are no easy feats. The development of new technologies is crucial to a continued space exploration program. In the next chapter, we'll take a look at what this might look like in the future!

BALLOON AEROSTAT

In this activity, you will design a balloon aerostat to take readings of air temperature. Try this experiment on a day with good weather.

❯ **Poke four small holes in the sides of a small cardboard box, near the top.** Tie small pieces of kite string through the holes, and then hang the box from the bottom of the helium balloon with the string. Tie one end of the remaining spool of kite string to the balloon.

❯ **Use the thermometer to record the temperature at ground level.** Write this number down in your science journal. Next, write a prediction in your science journal. Will the ground temperature or the air temperature be warmer?

❯ **Put the thermometer in the box and let out the kite string so that the balloon rises as high as it can—but still hold on to the string!** Let the balloon hang at the end of the string so that the thermometer will record the temperature at the higher elevation.

❯ **Pull the string in as quickly as you can, bringing down the balloon and thermometer. Has the temperature changed?** Is it cooler on the ground or in the air? Write down the temperature in your science journal. Compare your results with your prediction.

Try This!

Create a table to organize your data. Your table should have three headings: date, ground temperature, and air temperature. During one week, take temperature readings at the same time of day and in the same area. At the end of the week, look at your results. What do your results tell you about air near the ground versus air higher up?

DESIGN A MARS ROVER

Imagine that you are a NASA engineer. How would you design a Mars rover? What equipment would your rover have? How would you make your rover stable? How would your rover land on the surface of Mars?

❯ **Brainstorm your ideas for a new Mars rover.** To begin, decide on the goal of the program so you know what features the rover needs to have to complete the goal. Is it meant to collect soil samples? Take photographs? Gather air samples? All of these?

❯ **Sketch your ideas in your science notebook.** Begin to decide on the supplies you'll use to build a model. Do you want materials that can move easily? Strong materials? Flexible materials?

❯ **Gather your supplies and begin to build your model.** Follow your designs, but don't be afraid to veer from your original drawings if you discover other ways of doing things.

❯ **When you have a finished model, test it.** Does it move the way you want it to? Is it capable of collecting the samples you need?

DID YOU KNOW?

In March 2018, Mars rover *Curiosity* celebrated 2,000 sols, or Mars days, on the planet!

Try This!

Was your design a success? Why or why not? Brainstorm in your science journal about what you could improve. Try out your ideas and see if they make a difference. Record your observations in your science journal.

ROCKET MARK I

Ideas for supplies: balloon, cardboard tube from paper towels or toilet paper, glue, scissors, construction paper, straw, thin stick that will fit loosely in the straw, science journal, and pencil

In this activity, you will make a model of a rocket. Your model will use pressurized air to provide the push. Do this activity with an adult.

Caution: Always launch your rocket in a wide-open space. Be certain to let everyone in the area know what is about to happen.

❯ **Place the balloon inside the tube, with the open end sticking out the bottom.** Put a drop of glue on the top of the balloon, and glue it to the inside of the tube near the top.

❯ **Cut three fins from construction paper.** Glue them to the sides of your tube near the bottom.

❯ **Cut a circle from construction paper, and then cut a triangle out of the circle, like a slice of pie.** Fold the circle into a cone and glue it together. Glue this to the top of your tube to make a nose cone.

❯ **Glue the straw to the side of the tube and let it dry.**

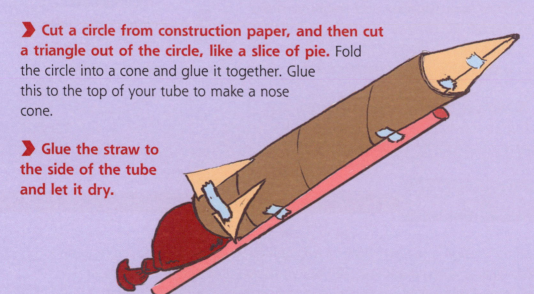

❯ **Place the stick in the ground, pointing straight up.** Blow up the balloon so it is pushing against the inside of the tube. It's okay if some of the balloon is sticking out the bottom. Pinch the end of the balloon closed, but don't tie it off. Place the rocket onto the stick by sliding the straw down onto it.

❯ **When you are ready, release the end of the balloon.** What happens? What forces are at work?

Try This!

How could you get your balloon to move faster? Try your idea and compare your results with your hypothesis. What do you think would happen if you added a weight to your balloon? Try and see. Note your observations and record your results in your science journal.

Operation Paperclip

During World War II, rocketry advanced more than ever before as countries used this technology to send bombs to other countries. Germany was especially advanced. At the end of the war, both the United States and the Soviet Union wanted the German scientists who held key knowledge about the superior German rocketry. Scientists were brought to the United States without State Department approval in a program with the code name Operation Paperclip. Through Operation Paperclip, almost 500 German scientists moved to the United States. The German scientists' expertise and the hardware from the German rockets helped the United States build the foundation of its rocketry and space travel programs.

MAKE A ROBOTIC LANDER

Build a model of the *Apollo 11 Lunar Module Eagle*. Do you think that you could have landed the *Eagle* on the moon? Test your pilot skills and your model's landing gear in this activity.

❯ **Take a small cardboard box and cut four diagonal slits in the top and bottom of the box at the four corners, about a third of the way along each side.** Cut one slit in each side, connecting one of the pairs of top and bottom slits. You should now have four corners that are only connected at one side. Fold these into the box, and tape in place, creating an **octagonal** box.

❯ **Cover the box, four drinking straws, four bottle caps,** and about three dozen toothpicks individually with gold Mylar film.

❯ **Build a landing leg with a straw and bottle cap.** Use toothpicks to make the leg stick out at an angle. What could you use instead of bottle caps and straws that would absorb the shock of landing on the moon?

❯ **Repeat the previous step three more times,** adding three more legs to the box. Cut the remaining toothpicks in half, and glue a few of them horizontally along to form a ladder. You have now finished the descent stage of the lunar module.

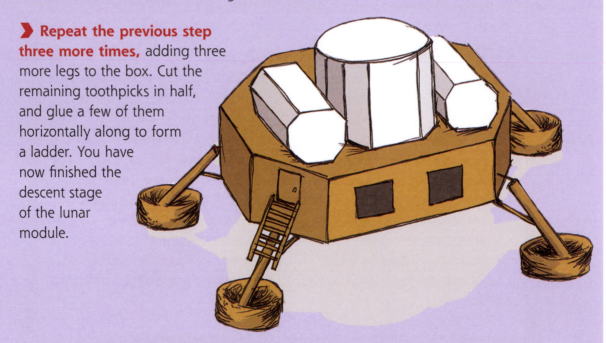

WORDS TO KNOW

octagonal: eight-sided.

> **Use the ascent templates to make the ascent stage from some white cardboard. You can find the templates at NomadPress.net/Templates.** Cover the ascent pieces in aluminum foil. Secure the ascent module on top of the descent module with glue.

> **With a black marker, add details to your lander.** You could draw the ingress/egress port (the NASA term for a door) above the ladder.

> **After building your new landing gear, drop your lander from a height no greater than one foot.** Does your lander stay upright? Record your results in your science journal.

Think About It

You have built a model of the *Eagle* lander. If NASA asked you to build a lander today, what would it look like? Sketch your ideas in your science journal. Explain why you created this design.

Lunar Reflectors

Astronauts with the *Apollo 11, 14,* and *15* missions left behind reflectors on the surface of the moon. The reflectors look like cube-shaped prisms. Each reflector has 100 mirrors. Astronauts positioned the reflectors to face Earth. From time to time, astronomers bounce laser beams off these reflectors from the earth. By measuring the time that it takes the beam to return, they can precisely measure the distance from the earth to the moon.

MAKE SOME SOLAR POWER!

In the future, solar cells could be used by spacecraft to explore farther and faster in space. In this activity, you will make a solar-powered vehicle. Where will your vehicle travel to?

Ideas for supplies: package of straws, aluminum foil, masking tape, plastic water bottle, water, hand drill, paper clip, craft sticks or disposable chopsticks, cardboard, scissors, small magnet, stiff electrical wire, small light bulb, rocks or blocks

Caution: Ask an adult to help you drill holes in the bottle cap and craft sticks.

❯ **Make six extra-long straws by pushing the end of one straw into another.** Tape six long straws together in a star pattern. Tape six other straws between the ends of the straws, making a web or net.

❯ **Cover the web with aluminum foil.** Try to keep it as smooth as possible. This is your solar reflector.

❯ **Fill a plastic bottle with water.** Wrap it in black plastic and place it in the middle of the reflector. The black plastic absorbs heat.

❯ **Take the cap off the plastic bottle.** Drill or punch a large hole in the cap, slightly off-center. It should be about the size of a pencil.

❯ **Drill small holes, the diameter of a paper clip, through two craft sticks.** The holes should be slightly toward one end. Tape the two craft sticks to either side of the cap, with the holes sticking up. They should be at a 90-degree angle to the offset hole in the cap.

❯ **Cut two small rectangles of cardboard, slightly less wide than the space between the two sticks and two inches long.** Cut a notch halfway through in the middle of both rectangles. Slip the two rectangles together at the notches, making an "X" shape.

❯ **Unbend a paper clip and slide it through the two holes in the craft sticks.** The clip should spin freely in the holes. Bend up one end of the clip so it will not slip out of the hole.

❯ **Tape the cardboard "X" to the metal paper clip.** One of the inside corners lays along the clip.

❯ **Wrap the other end of the paper clip around a small magnet and tape it in place.** Screw the lid back on the bottle.

❯ **Tape the middle part of a long piece of wire to the end of the stick.** Coil the wire into several round coils surrounding, but not touching, the magnet. The magnet should spin freely within the coils, so the coils need to be far enough away from the magnet to allow that.

❯ **Attach the two other ends of the wire to the small light bulb.** One wire should touch the base of the bulb and the other should touch the threads on the side.

❯ **Place the entire project in sunlight.** Fold up the sides of the reflector so that the sunlight hits the plastic bottle. If you need to, prop up the sides of the reflector with rocks or blocks to keep it aimed at the bottle. The sunlight will heat up the water in the bottle, creating steam. The steam will escape from the large hole, spinning the cardboard fan. This will turn the magnet within the metal coils, which will generate an electrical charge in the wire, lighting the bulb.

Try This!

You can experiment with powering other electrical devices, such as a small radio, with your solar-powered generator. Write down your ideas and results in your science journal.

Chapter 7

FUTURE SPACE
EXPLORATION

As you have learned, rockets have the power to send spacecraft into Earth's orbit. They have already taken astronauts to the moon and back. The now retired space shuttles used rockets, too. Each shuttle carried more than 1 million pounds of solid fuel!

Space agencies such as NASA and private companies such as SpaceX and Blue Origin are working on new types of heavy rockets. A heavy rocket could carry more weight and travel farther than ever before. Currently, the *Falcon Heavy* from SpaceX is the most powerful rocket in the world. While a space shuttle could carry loads up to 53,790 pounds, the *Falcon Heavy* could carry up to 140,660 pounds! The goal of the *Falcon Heavy*'s design team is to reach Mars by 2022.

ESSENTIAL QUESTION

How might people use sails and space elevators in the future?

The *Falcon Heavy* is one example of the innovative strategies designers are using to allow people to explore the farthest reaches of space. Let's take a look at some of the other ideas!

SAILS

Sails might be another possible solution for long space voyages. The sails could be made of a thin reflective material that unfolded after the spacecraft launched. The spacecraft would be propelled forward by the solar wind. The solar wind isn't like the winds on Earth. Wind on Earth is caused by changes in the temperature of the air in the atmosphere.

The solar wind is a constant stream of charged particles that flows outward from the sun.

The *Falcon Heavy* on the launch pad

credit: SpaceX

101

WORDS TO KNOW

corona: the outermost part of the sun's atmosphere.

termination shock: the point at which particles traveling outward from the sun slow to below the speed of sound.

NASA and the Japan Aerospace Exploration Agency (JAXA) have successfully tested solar sails. On May 21, 2010, JAXA launched the first solar sail probe, *IKAROS*, into space. Its solar sail, measuring 45 by 65 feet when open, had a thin film of solar cells. Energy from sunlight bouncing off the cells pushed the probe forward. It was even able to fly by Venus!

DID YOU KNOW?

The *IKAROS* probe was named after a character in Greek mythology called Icarus who flew too close to the sun with wax wings. The wings melted, and Icarus fell into the sea and drowned. *IKAROS* did not have this problem!

A 20-meter solar sail and boom system
credit: NASA/Marshall Space Flight Center

In 2015, NASA tested a solar sail nicknamed "Windjammer" after a science fiction story by Arthur C. Clarke (1917–2008) about a solar sailing competition. The folded sail weighed 110 pounds and was only the size of a dishwasher, but when unfurled it was almost one-quarter the size of a football field!

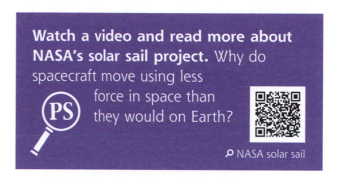

Watch a video and read more about NASA's solar sail project. Why do spacecraft move using less force in space than they would on Earth?

PS

🔎 NASA solar sail

In 2016, NASA began testing an electric sail, or e-sail, invented by the Finnish scientist Pekka Janhunen. The proposed spacecraft would have multiple wires radiating out in all directions. The wires would be about 12 miles long and as thin as paper clips! Protons in the solar wind would be repelled by the positively charged wires and push the spacecraft forward. The sail could reach speeds up to 93 miles a second! With speeds such as this, a spacecraft could exit our solar system in less than 10 years.

Solar Wind

The solar wind is a stream of plasma escaping from the sun's hot **corona**. The plasma stretches for millions of miles into space in all directions. The solar wind flows toward Earth at about 1 million miles per hour!

The solar wind doesn't travel that fast all the time, however. It slows down as it travels away from the sun. Eventually, the solar wind passes through the interstellar medium—an area of space between the star systems that contains gas and dust. The solar wind then slows down to about 94 AUs from the sun. At this point, the wind is going about the speed of sound. This point is called the **termination shock**. The *Voyager 1* spacecraft crossed the termination shock in 2004. Three years later, *Voyager 2* passed this point.

railgun: a device that uses electromagnetic force to launch projectiles.

counterweight: a weight that balances another weight.

RAILGUNS AND SPACE ELEVATORS

Before we can send a spacecraft to the moon, Mars, or anywhere else in the solar system, we must get it off the earth. This takes a great deal of energy. Most of a rocket's fuel energy is used to propel a spacecraft away from Earth. Much less energy is needed to push the ship toward its goal.

An artist's concept of a space elevator
credit: NASA/Pat Rawlings

Traditionally, we have used rockets to get objects into space, either to put them in orbit around the earth or to send them to other parts of the solar system. Other methods could be used instead of rockets, such as magnetic **railguns**, sometimes called magnetic rail launchers. A railgun uses magnetic force to propel an object.

In the future, railguns could launch people and cargo from the moon or Mars if we set up permanent bases there. Both Mars and the moon have less gravity than the earth, so railguns would need less energy to launch objects.

DID YOU KNOW?

The idea for a space elevator was first dreamed up in 1895 by Konstantin Tsiolkovsky, a Russian scientist who did pioneering work in rocketry.

Another idea for lifting spaceships, cargo, and people off a planet and into orbit is a space elevator. The idea of a space elevator was first suggested by Russian rocket scientist, Konstantin Tsiolkovsky (1857–1935) in 1895. The elevator could be made of a very long, very strong series of cables. One end would be attached to the earth, probably near the equator, in a country such as Brazil or Ecuador. The other end would be attached to a large satellite. The space elevator would lift its cargo into space by using motors to climb the cable, or it could use a system of **counterweights**. Gravity would help the elevator on the way down.

Space elevators could make it cheaper to put cargo and people in space.

ESSENTIAL QUESTION

How might people use sails and space elevators in the future?

The solar system is a vast, remarkable place that we have only begun to explore. What scientific wonders are waiting for us as we develop the technology necessary to travel farther and farther afield? Will you be the one to step foot on another planet?

MAGNETIC RAIL LAUNCHER

Will there be a railway into space? Imagine that you are part of a team of NASA engineers working on a track to launch spacecraft into orbit. In this activity, you will design a model of a magnetic rail launcher.

❯ **Cut a straw in half lengthwise.** This will be your rail. Cut out two saddle-shaped cardboard supports and tape them to either end of the rail. Put the rail on top of a large piece of cardboard and tape it in place.

❯ **Make an electromagnet.** Wrap electrical wire around a nail as many times as will fit. Tape one end of the wire to one end of a battery. Run the other end to a paper clip. Tape a second piece of wire from the other end of the battery to underneath the paper clip. Tape a piece of cardboard on the paper clip so that you can touch the clip—to make a button. Bend the clip so that when you press down on the button, the **circuit** will connect, magnetizing the nail. Make two more electromagnets just like the first.

❯ **Cut a small, straight piece of paper clip and lay it across one end of your rail.** Place one electromagnet underneath the rail at just the right distance so that when you connect the circuit, the piece of paper clip will be pulled toward the magnet.

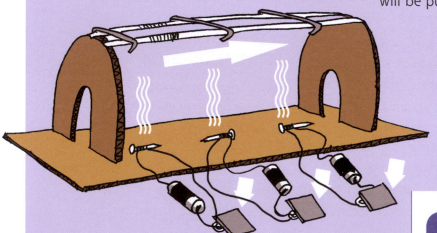

WORDS TO KNOW

electromagnet: metal made into a magnet by passing electric current through it.

circuit: a path for electric current to flow, beginning and ending at the same point.

> **Place the next two electromagnets under the rail at a similar distance down the rail** so that when they are turned on, they pull the piece of paper clip farther down.

> **Place the three buttons for the three electromagnets next to each other** so that you can quickly press them one after another. Tape them in place.

> **Practice pushing your buttons in order so that as soon as the clip has been pulled to one magnet,** that first one turns off and the next one comes on. This may take some practice to get right. In time, you should be able to get the clip to quickly zip from one end of the rail to the other, and even off the end. Write down your observations in your science journal.

Think More

You just built a model of a magnetic rail launcher. Were you able to get your launcher working smoothly? How could you improve your design?

Ride the Maglev!

Magnetic rails aren't just for space travel! You can ride on a magnetic rail here on Earth! These trains are called maglev trains (short for magnetic levitation) and they operate on the same basic principal as the ones that might someday shoot us into space. With maglev trains, two sets of magnets are used: one to push the train up from the rail so it's floating slightly above the track, and another to propel the train along. These trains can accelerate and decelerate much more quickly that traditional trains, and they are very energy-efficient.

BUILD A SOLAR WIND-POWERED SPACECRAFT

In this activity, you will design a solar wind-powered spacecraft to experiment with sun and wind power.

❯ **First, make wheels for your spacecraft.** Take a plastic yogurt cup lid and lay it on a piece of cardboard. Trace around it with a pencil four times, creating four circles. Cut them out and glue them inside four yogurt cup lids.

❯ **Poke four holes in the sides of a small cardboard box, two on the bottom near the front and on opposite sides of the box, and two at the back, also opposite each other.** Make sure the holes are in a straight line across the box from each other. They also need to be big enough to fit a pair of dowels so they can spin freely. Slide the dowels through the holes.

▶ **Cut holes in the centers of the wheels and slide them on the ends of the dowels.** Glue them in place.

▶ **Make a hole in the top of the box big enough to fit a straw.** Stick a straw in it. Tape six other straws to the top of this straw, radiating away from the first one like a star or web.

▶ **Tape plastic wrap over the straws, creating a sail.** Place your craft on a flat surface. Aim a fan or hair dryer at the sail and turn it on. Watch your craft go. Run behind it with the fan or hair dryer, keeping up the push of the "solar wind."

DID YOU KNOW?

Even traveling as fast as the fastest current spaceship, at 50,000 miles an hour, it would take more than 50,000 years to reach the nearest star, Proxima Centauri.

Think More

Researchers in the United States are working on a new way for spacecraft to travel using an electric sail or e-sail. The electric sail would be powered by protons in the solar wind. In your science journal, sketch and write down ideas for a space sail design. Think about the materials you could use and the shape of the sail.

Read and see illustrations of a space sail here.

🔍 Space interstellar solar sails

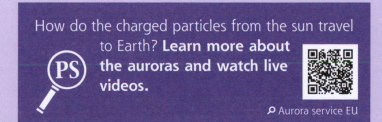

How do the charged particles from the sun travel to Earth? **Learn more about the auroras and watch live videos.**

🔍 Aurora service EU

A SPACE ELEVATOR

Ideas for supplies: bucket, dirt or sand, broomstick or other long thin stick, 2 empty thread spools, 3 long nails, hammer, 2 empty soup cans, string, payload such as pennies or blocks, science journal, and pencil

Use your engineering skills to design a space elevator and then test how much weight it can lift.

Caution: Ask an adult to help you poke holes in the cans.

❯ **Fill a bucket with dirt or sand.** Stick one end of a broomstick into the sand so it stands straight up.

❯ **Hammer two nails into the side of the broomstick.** Nail one near the top of the stick. Nail the other one into the bottom of the stick near the top of the dirt. Put one spool on each of the nails. You are making **pulleys** from these.

❯ **With the hammer and another nail, poke a hole in the center of the bottom of two empty soup cans.** Poke two holes in opposite sides of the top of each can. Thread a piece of string through the two top holes and tie it off, creating a handle for the can.

90,000 Miles Tall

Some scientists are looking at building a space elevator that might be more than 90,000 miles tall. Such an elevator could reduce the cost of putting things in space to a fraction of the current price. Since the top pulley would be a satellite in Earth's orbit, no giant broomstick like in your model would be necessary. Only the strings and giant cables would be needed.

WORDS TO KNOW

pulley: a wheel through which a cord passes, used to lift heavy objects.

Activity

❯ **Hook the handle of one of the cans around the nail at the top of the stick.** (This is temporary.) Thread one end of a string through the hole at the bottom of this can. Tie a knot in the end of the string coming out the top, so that it won't pass through the hole. Run the other end down the stick and wrap it once around the spool at the bottom. Place the second can at the bottom of the stick. Then, push the end of the string through the hole in the bottom of the second can, and tie it off with a knot as well.

❯ **Take another string and tie it around the handle of the bottom can.** Run it up the stick and wrap it once around the top spool. Unhook the first can from the spool and tie the end of the string to the handle of the top can.

❯ **Load one can with your payload.** Load the other can at the top with enough dirt to balance the weight of the load in the bottom can. What do you notice about the position of the cans when they are balanced? It should take only a slight push to move the elevator up or down.

Think More

One danger that space elevator engineers must tackle are potential collisions with floating space debris such as satellites. In your science journal, write down possible ways that the elevator could avoid collisions with space debris.

In 2007, NASA held a student competition. Teams from all over the world built space elevator prototypes. **Watch a video about the space elevator here.**

PS

🔍 Nova YouTube space elevator

accelerate: to change the speed of an object through time.

accretion: the process of particles sticking together to form larger objects, such as asteroids or planets.

aerostat: an aerial robot. Also called aerobot.

Anasazi: an ancient civilization of the American Southwest.

asteroid: a small rocky object orbiting the sun. Asteroids are too small to be planets.

astrolabe: a tool used for calculating the altitude of objects in the sky.

astronomer: a person who studies the stars, planets, and other objects in space.

astronomical: having to do with astronomy or the study of space.

astronomical unit (AU): a unit of measure used in space. One AU is the average distance from the earth to the sun, 93 million miles.

astrophysicist: a person who studies what makes up the stars and universe.

atmosphere: the mixture of gases that surrounds a planet.

atom: the smallest particle of matter.

axis: an imaginary line through a planet's poles, around which it rotates. Plural is axes.

BCE: put after a date, BCE stands for Before Common Era and counts down to zero. CE stands for Common Era and counts up from zero. These non-religious terms correspond to BC and AD. This book was printed in 2019 CE.

Big Bang: an explosion that led to the beginning of the universe.

carbon: an element found in all living things.

carbon dioxide (CO_2): a gas in the air made of carbon and oxygen atoms.

celestial object: a star, planet, moon, or other object in space, such as an asteroid or comet.

circuit: a path for electric current to flow, beginning and ending at the same point.

civilization: a community of people that is advanced in art, science, and government.

classify: to put things in groups based on what they have in common.

climate change: a change in long-term weather patterns, which can happen through natural or man-made processes.

comet: a small, icy object formed in the outer solar system that can emit tails of gas and dust if it approaches the sun.

concave: a surface that curves inward like the inside of a bowl.

constellation: a group of stars that form a shape or pattern. There are 88 official constellations in the sky.

convection: the transfer of heat from one region to another by the movement of a gas or liquid.

convex: a surface that curves outward like the outside of a bowl.

core: the center.

corona: the outermost part of the sun's atmosphere.

counterweight: a weight that balances another weight.

crater: a large, bowl-shaped hole on a planet or moon.

crust: the outer, thin layer of the earth.

data: information, facts, and numbers from tests and experiments.

debris: the scattered pieces of something that has been broken or destroyed.

dense: when something is tightly packed in its space.

distort: to make something look different from its normal shape.

dwarf planet: similar to a planet but not massive enough to clear its orbit of other, similar objects.

electromagnetic: one of the fundamental forces of the universe. It is responsible for magnetic attraction and electrical charges.

electromagnet: metal made into a magnet by passing electric current through it.

electron: a small particle that makes up atoms. It has a negative charge and exists outside the nucleus.

element: a pure substance that is made of atoms that are all the same.

elliptical: shaped like an ellipse, or an oval.

engineer: a person who uses science, math, and creativity to design and build things.

erosion: the process of wearing down Earth's surface, usually by water, wind, or ice.

GLOSSARY

evaporate: when a liquid heats up and changes into a gas.

exoplanet: a planet that orbits a star other than the sun.

fossil: the remains or traces of ancient plants or animals left in rock.

friction: a force that slows down objects when they rub against each other.

fuse: to join together under high heat.

galaxy: a collection of star systems.

gamma ray: light that has the shortest wavelength and highest energy.

generator: a machine that converts energy into electricity.

geocentric: the belief, now disproved, that the earth is the center of the solar system.

geology: the study of the earth and its rocks. A scientist who studies geology is a geologist.

geometry: a branch of mathematics that deals with points, lines, and shapes and where they are in space.

Global Positioning System (GPS): a system of satellites, computers, and receivers that can determine the exact location of a receiver anywhere on the planet.

gravity: a force that pulls all matter together, including planets, moons, and stars.

gravity well: the pull of gravity that a large object in space exerts.

greenhouse effect: a process through which energy from the sun is trapped by a planet's atmosphere, warming it.

heliocentric: the belief that the sun is the center of the solar system.

helium: the second most common element in the universe after hydrogen.

hydrogen: a colorless gas that is the most abundant gas in the universe.

impact crater: a crater formed when an object such as an asteroid slams into the surface of another object in space.

indigenous: native to a place.

ion: an atom with a positive or negative electrical charge. This means it has an extra electron or is missing an electron.

iron: an element that is a common metal.

Jovian planets: a term for Jupiter, Saturn, Uranus, Neptune.

Kuiper Belt: a large belt of comets and asteroids that orbits the sun in an area at about 100 AU.

Kuiper Belt Objects (KBOs): planetoids and dwarf planets, such as Pluto and Eris, that exist in the Kuiper Belt.

lava: magma that has risen to the earth's surface.

lifespan: the average expected length of time from birth to death.

light-year: the distance light travels in one year, about 5.9 trillion miles.

lithium: a metal.

long-period comet: a comet with an orbit longer than 200 years.

magma: a mixture of molten, semi-molten, and solid rock beneath Earth's surface.

magnesium: an element that is abundant in nature.

mantle: the layer of the earth between the crust and the core, the upper portion of which is partially molten.

mare: a dark area on Earth's moon. Plural is maria.

mass: the amount of matter in an object.

matter: what an object is made of. Anything that has weight and takes up space.

meteor: a rock or chunk of ice that falls toward Earth from space. Small meteors burn up before they reach Earth and we see them as shooting stars.

meteorite: a piece of rock that falls from space and lands on Earth's surface.

meteoroid: a piece of dust or rock orbiting around the sun.

methane: a colorless, odorless gas that burns easily.

molten: melted into liquid by heat.

momentum: the force that a moving object has in the direction that it is moving.

NASA: National Aeronautics and Space Administration, the U.S. organization in charge of space exploration.

nebula: a giant cloud of gas and dust among the stars. Plural is nebulae.

neutron: a particle that makes up atoms. It is in the nucleus and has no charge.

neutron star: a star that has collapsed under its gravity and whose atoms have all converted to neutrons.

newton: a unit used to measure the amount of force you need to move something.

nickel: a hard, silver element.

nuclear fusion: when hydrogen fuses into helium, producing energy and light.

nuclear power: power produced by splitting atoms.

nucleus: the central part of an atom, made up of protons and neutrons.

nutrients: substances in food and soil that living things need to live and grow.

observatory: a place from which astronomers can observe the planets, stars, and galaxies.

octagonal: eight-sided.

Oort Cloud: a huge collection of comets that orbit around the outer regions of the solar system.

orbit: the path an object in space takes around a star, planet, or moon.

oxygen: a gas in the air that people and animals need to breathe to stay alive.

Pangaea: a huge supercontinent that existed about 300 million years ago. It contained all the land on Earth.

parallax: the apparent change in position of a star compared to the stars behind it, as viewed from one side of the earth's orbit around the sun and compared to the view from the other side, half a year later.

patent: having the exclusive right to make, use, or sell something.

perpendicular: when an object forms a right angle with another object.

phenomenon: something seen or observed. Plural is phenomena.

physics: the study of physical forces, including matter, energy, and motion, and how these forces interact with each other.

planet: a large body in space that orbits the sun and does not produce its own light. There are eight planets.

planetoid: a small celestial object resembling a planet.

plasma: a form of matter that is similar to gas.

probe: a spaceship or other device used to explore outer space.

propulsion: pushing or moving an object forward.

proton: a particle that makes up atoms. It is in the nucleus and has a positive charge.

pulley: a wheel through which a cord passes, used to lift heavy objects.

pulsar: a neutron star that rotates and emits energy, appearing to pulse as it rotates.

radiation: the process by which energy such as light or sound moves from its source and radiates outward.

radioactive: having or producing a powerful form of energy known as radioactivity.

radio astronomy: a branch of astronomy that uses giant radio antennas to detect radiation emitted from astronomical objects.

radio wave: an electromagnetic wave used for sending radio or television signals through the air.

railgun: a device that uses electromagnetic force to launch projectiles.

refracting telescope: a telescope with a lens that gathers light and forms an image of something far away.

remnant: a small, leftover piece of something.

retrograde rotation: rotating in the opposite direction of normal.

robotics: the science of designing, building, controlling, and operating robots.

rotation: turning around a fixed point.

rover: a slow-moving vehicle used to explore planets.

satellite: a natural or artificial object that orbits a larger object in space.

science fiction: a story featuring imaginary science and technology.

seismic: relating to earthquakes.

seismometer: an instrument used to detect and record movement and vibration in the earth or other objects. Also called a seismograph.

short-period comet: a comet with an orbit shorter than 200 years.

silicon: a nonmetallic element found in clay and sand that is used to make computer parts.

solar cell: a device that converts the energy of the sun into electrical energy.

solar eclipse: when the moon passes between the sun and the earth.

solar system: the sun, the eight planets, and their moons, together with smaller bodies. The planets orbit the sun.

solar wind: the stream of electrically charged particles emitted by the sun.

Soviet Union: a former country that included present-day Russia.

Space Race: the competition between the United States and the Soviet Union to achieve the greatest accomplishments in space exploration.

spectrometer: an instrument used to study the properties of light.

speculate: to make a guess or theory about something without having all the information.

sphere: a three-dimensional round shape, like a ball.

supernova: the explosion of a giant star.

tectonic plate: a large section of the earth's crust that moves on top of the mantle, the layer beneath the crust.

temperate: climate or weather that is not extreme.

termination shock: the point at which particles traveling outward from the sun slow to below the speed of sound.

terrestrial planet: one of the four planets closest to the sun—Mercury, Venus, Earth, and Mars. All share characteristics with Earth.

Trojan War: a war fought between the ancient Greeks and the people of Troy around 1250 BCE.

ultraviolet ray: a type of light with a shorter wavelength than visible light, also called black light.

universe: everything that exists, everywhere.

uranium: a naturally radioactive element.

volcanism: the motion of molten rock under a planet's surface, which results in volcanos.

wane: to get smaller.

water vapor: water as a gas, such as fog, steam, or mist.

wax: to get bigger.

Metric Conversions

Use this chart to find the metric equivalents to the English measurements in this book. If you need to know a half measurement, divide by two. If you need to know twice the measurement, multiply by two. How do you find a quarter measurement? How do you find three times the measurement?

English	Metric
1 inch	2.5 centimeters
1 foot	30.5 centimeters
1 yard	0.9 meter
1 mile	1.6 kilometers
1 pound	0.5 kilogram
1 teaspoon	5 milliliters
1 tablespoon	15 milliliters
1 cup	237 milliliters

BOOKS

Aguilar, David A. *13 Planets: The Latest View of the Solar System.* National Geographic, 2011.

Aguilar, David A. *Seven Wonders of the Solar System.* Viking, 2017.

Carson, Mary Kay. *Beyond the Solar System: Exploring Galaxies, Black Holes, Alien Planets, and More: a History with 21 Activities.* Chicago Review Press, 2013.

DeCristofano, Carolyn Cinami. *A Black Hole Is Not a Hole.* Turtleback Books, 2017.

Scott, Elaine. *Space, Stars, and the Beginning of Time: What the Hubble Telescope Saw.* Houghton Mifflin Harcourt, 2018.

Shetterly, Margot Lee. *Hidden Figures: Young Readers' Edition.* HarperCollins, 2016.

Simon, Seymour. *Our Solar System.* HarperCollins, 2014.

Yasuda, Anita. *Explore Comets and Asteroids.* Nomad Press, 2017.

Yasuda, Anita. *Astronomy: Cool Women in Space.* Nomad Press, 2015.

Wood, Matthew Brenden. *The Space Race: How the Cold War Put Humans on the Moon.* Nomad Press, 2018.

WEBSITES

Amateur Telescope Makers: *atm-workshop.com*

Astronomy Magazine: *astronomy.com*

European Space Agency (ESA) Space for Kids: *esa.int/esaKIDSen*

In-the-Sky Satellite Tracking: *in-the-sky.org/satmap_worldmap.php*

NASA for Students: *nasa.gov/audience/forstudents/index.html*

NASA–Search for Planets: *planetquest.jpl.nasa.gov/index.cfm*

The Planetary Society: *planetary.org/home*

Space.com: *space.com*

MUSEUMS AND PLANETARIUMS

Adler Planetarium and Astronomy Museum, Chicago, IL: *adlerplanetarium.org*

American Museum of Natural History, New York, NY: *amnh.org*

Buffalo Museum of Science Buffalo, Buffalo, NY: *sciencebuff.org*

California Science Center, Los Angeles, CA: *californiasciencecenter.org*

Center of Science and Industry, Columbus, OH: *cosi.org*

Denver Museum of Nature and Science, Denver, CO: *dmns.org*

Kopernik Observatory and Science Education Center, Vestal, NY: *kopernik.org*

Houston Museum of Natural Science, Houston, TX: *hmns.org*

Lawrence Hall of Science, Berkeley, CA: *lawrencehallofscience.org*

Miami Museum of Science and Planetarium, Miami, FL: *miamisci.org*

Montshire Museum of Science, Norwich, VT: *montshire.org*

RESOURCES

MUSEUMS AND PLANETARIUMS (Continued)

Museum of Science, Boston, MA: *mos.org*

Museum of Science and Industry, Chicago, IL: *msichicago.org*

New Mexico Museum of Natural History and Science, Albuquerque, NM: *nmnaturalhistory.org/visitors/planetarium*

Pacific Science Center, Seattle, WA: *pacsci.org*

Reuben H. Fleet Science Center, San Diego, CA: *rhfleet.org*

Saint Louis Science Center, St. Louis, MO: *slsc.org*

Science Museum of Virginia, Richmond, VA: *smv.org*

Smithsonian National Air and Space Museum, Washington, DC: *nasm.si.edu*

QR CODE GLOSSARY

page 7: *youtube.com/watch?v=5AAR7bNSM_s*

page 13: *imagine.gsfc.nasa.gov/educators/lessons/xray_spectra/background-lifecycles.html*

page 16: *herschel.caltech.edu/page/about*

page 16: *esa.int/Our_Activities/Space_Science/Herschel*

page 20: *nasa.gov/mission_pages/chandra/multimedia/planetary_nebula.html*

page 23: *space.com/26894-living-on-mercury-explained-infographic.html*

page 27: *youtube.com/watch?v=VYMjSuleOBw*

page 30: *solarsystem.nasa.gov/moons/jupiter-moons/overview/?page=0&per_page=40&order=name+asc&search=&placeholder=Enter+moon+name&condition_1=9%3Aparent_id&condition_2=moon%3Abody_type%3Ailike&condition_3=moon%3Abody_type*

page 31: *spaceplace.nasa.gov/review/dr-marc-solar-system/gas-giants.html*

page 33: *solarsystem.nasa.gov/missions/cassini/science/rings*

page 35: *lasp.colorado.edu/education/outerplanets/giantplanets_whatandwhere.php*

page 36: *virtualmuseum.ca/edu/ViewLoitLo.do?method=preview&lang=EN&id=5185*

page 37: *mars.jpl.nasa.gov/gallery/atlas/olympus-mons.html*

page 38: *esa.int/Our_Activities/Space_Science/Venus_Express/Orbiter_instruments*

page 44: *airandspace.si.edu/research/projects/radar-mapping*

page 47: *spaceplace.nasa.gov/craters/en*

page 53: *solarsystem.nasa.gov/solar-system/kuiper-belt/overview*

page 55: *nasa.gov/mission_pages/newhorizons/videos/index.html*

page 59: *hubblesite.org/hubble_discoveries/comet_ison/blogs/great-moments-in-comet-history-comet-halley*

page 62: *dawn-mission.org*

page 65: *google.com/search?q=youtube+crab+nebula+nasa&rlz=1C1CHBF_enUS773US773&oq=youtube+crab+nebula+nasa&aqs=chrome..69i57j69i60.5925j0j7&sourceid=chrome&ie=UTF-8*

RESOURCES

ESSENTIAL QUESTIONS

Introduction: What is the solar system and how does it impact you?

Chapter 1: How did stars and planets form in the solar system?

Chapter 2: How are the terrestrial planets and Jovian planets similar? How are they different?

Chapter 3: How are the two types of craters made?

Chapter 4: Why do some astronomical objects remain undiscovered for so many centuries?

Chapter 5: How did the telescope change astronomers' views of the solar system?

Chapter 6: Why can't spacecraft simply carry their fuel onboard?

Chapter 7: How might people use sails and space elevators in the future?

INDEX

INDEX